Buried money secrets

The Hidden Loopholes, Wealth Tactics, and Financial Codes They Hide From You

Codex Occulto

© **Copyright 2025 by Codex Occulto - All rights reserved.**

This publication provides accurate and reliable information on the subject matter discussed. It is sold with the understanding that the publisher is not offering legal, accounting, or professional services. For such advice, consult a qualified expert.

No part of this document may be copied, reproduced, stored, or shared—electronically or in print—without written permission from the publisher. All rights reserved.

The content is presented as-is, with no guarantees. The publisher assumes no responsibility for any loss, damage, or consequences resulting from the use or misuse of the information provided.

Trademarks mentioned are the property of their respective owners and are used for identification purposes only. This publication is not affiliated with them.

All copyrights remain with their respective authors unless held by the publisher.
ISBN: 979-8-89965-384-1
Imprint: Staten House

Staten House

Table of Contents

Introduction - What They Never Wanted You to Know 9

Why the Rules Are Different for the Rich 9

Understanding the System You Were Never Taught 10

Who "They" Are and Why They Play a Different Game 11

How This Book Will Shift Your Financial Trajectory 12

Chapter 1 – The Two Financial Systems: One for Them, One for You 15

The Illusion of Fairness 15

How the Wealthy Bypass the Rules You Follow 17

Information Asymmetry: The Rich Have Access You Don't 19

The Real Purpose of Financial Education (Hint: It's Not for You) 22

Chapter 2 – Hidden Entities: How the Rich Protect Assets You'll Never See 26

Shell Corporations, Trusts, and Offshore Accounts 26

The Invisible Family Office 29

Why the Elite Avoid Personal Ownership 31

Secrets of Holding Companies and Asset Layers 34

Chapter 3 – The Art of Tax Disappearance: Legal Evasion vs. Smart Avoidance 39

Why the Ultra-Wealthy Pay Less (or Nothing) 39

Loopholes in Real Estate, Agriculture, and Foundations 41

Dynasty Trusts and Generation-Skipping Strategies 44

The Role of Charitable Trusts and Nonprofits in Tax Shielding 46

Chapter 4 – Debt Alchemy: Using Other People's Money Like the

Billionaires Do 52

    Why Debt Is Power in the Elite Playbook 52

    Leveraging Assets Without Selling Them 53

    Strategic Credit: Business Lines, Private Banking, and Collateralized Loans... 55

    The Difference Between "Good" Debt and "Manipulated" Debt 57

Chapter 5 – The Private Deal Pipeline: Where the Real Wealth Happens 61

    Angel Networks, Syndicates, and Pre-IPO Access 61

    Private Equity and Venture Capital for the Inner Circle 63

    How the Rich Buy Cash Flow, Not Jobs 66

    Why You'll Never Hear About the Best Investments (Until It's Too Late).... 68

Chapter 6 – Invisible Income Streams: Quiet Money They Don't Talk About 72

    Licensing, Royalties, and Intellectual Property Tricks 72

    Asset Leasing, Private Lending, and Hidden Passive Income 73

    How the Wealthy Turn Hobbies Into Write-Offs 75

    Secret Uses of Life Insurance for Wealth Transfer and Borrowing 77

Chapter 7 – Privacy as Power: How the Wealthy Erase Their Tracks 81

    How to Vanish Financially Without Breaking the Law 81

    The Power of Nominee Structures and Privacy Jurisdictions 83

    Financial Obfuscation: Making Yourself a Small Target 85

    Architecting the Ghost Profile 87

Chapter 8 – The Psychological Codes of the Elite 91

    Thinking in Net Worth, Not Income 91

    Delayed Gratification Is a Myth (Used Against You) 93

    Playing Long-Term Games with Unfair Advantages 94

Why the Wealthy Stay Quiet About Wealth 96

Chapter 9 – Breaking In: How You Start Using These Tactics Without a Fortune 100

Where to Begin With Limited Capital 100

The Power of Structure Before Scale 101

Leveraging Information, Relationships, and Access 103

What You Need to Unlearn—and What to Master Next 105

The Game Is Rigged - Play It Anyway 109

Mindset + Structure = Escape 111

What You Do With This Information Will Define Your Legacy 113

Recap for Essential Information 118

Fork in the Road 118

Ignore "Perfect Plan" Paralysis 118

12-Month "Structure Sprint" 118

Behavioral Inheritance 119

Downside Shields 119

Early-Structure Signaling 119

Quarterly Scorecard 120

Compound Bricks in a Dynasty Wall 120

Urgency Over Prediction 120

Raw Code Recap 120

Blank Page Choice 121

48-Hour Micro-Commitment 121

Success KPI Shift 121

Open-Door Reality 121

Final Directive.. 121

Introduction - What They Never Wanted You to Know

Why the Rules Are Different for the Rich

There's a hard truth that almost no one wants to admit: the rich play by a completely different set of rules than everyone else—and those rules are not written in any textbook, school curriculum, or mainstream financial advice column. What you've been taught about money is a sanitized version of reality, designed to keep you obedient, not sovereign.

For decades, the middle class has been sold the same dream: get an education, get a job, save diligently, avoid debt, and retire comfortably. It's a tidy narrative. It offers hope. It creates compliance. But it doesn't build wealth.

That path is a trap—an outdated formula built on assumptions that no longer hold. Inflation eats your savings. Job security is a myth. And while you're told to cut back on lattes and budget responsibly, the wealthy are legally parking millions offshore, borrowing against appreciating assets to fund their lifestyles tax-free, and using layers of corporate structures to funnel income without ever receiving a "salary."

They don't clip coupons or argue over tax refunds. They erase tax obligations before they're even calculated.

It's not that the game is rigged—it's that you've been handed the wrong rulebook. You were trained for a game called "personal finance." But the elite don't play that game. They play **structured finance**—a higher-order version with tools, loopholes, and legal shields you were never meant to learn.

The rich don't work for money. They make money work for them. They don't "earn" income—they generate returns. And they don't pay taxes like you do, because they don't structure their lives around salaries—they structure around equity, trusts, depreciation, and debt.

These aren't secrets because they're hidden—they're secrets because nobody in power has dared to teach them to you. Because the truth is dangerous. If everyone understood how money moves, the system would collapse under the weight of its inequality.

But now, you're about to understand. And once you see it, you can't go back.

Understanding the System You Were Never Taught

What most people think of as "the financial system" is only the surface layer: checking accounts, credit cards, 401(k)s, insurance plans, and mortgages. These are the tools designed for the masses—easy to understand, easy to tax, easy to control.

Beneath that, however, is a deeper, more sophisticated ecosystem—one reserved for those with the knowledge, connections, and capital to use it. This isn't a conspiracy. It's structure. And the people who live in that world aren't smarter. They're simply informed. They have access to a private operating system—a financial architecture most people will never see.

This hidden system includes:

- **Legal entities** that separate control from liability
- **Trusts** that protect wealth from taxes, lawsuits, and governments
- **Jurisdictions** that reward invisibility, privacy, and protection
- **Tax structures** that allow money to move, grow, and compound untaxed
- **Credit lines** that replace income with tax-free liquidity
- **Family offices** that operate as silent empires

The deeper you look, the clearer it becomes: wealth is not about how much you earn. It's about how you structure, protect, and leverage what you control.

You've likely heard the phrase "knowledge is power." But in finance, power comes from exclusive knowledge—applied knowledge. Not what's on the news. Not what your HR department offers. Not what your financial advisor learned in a weekend course. Real wealth knowledge lives in boardrooms, law firms, and family office briefings—circles you were never invited into.

The wealthy don't chase yield. They engineer outcomes. They don't ask for permission. They create systems that produce permanent advantages.

You were never taught this. Not in school. Not in college. Not even by your "trusted" financial institutions. Why?

Because your ignorance is profitable.

The more you believe that wealth comes from saving harder, working longer, or buying index funds, the easier it is for the real players to extract value from you. You are the customer, the taxpayer, the labor. The gears of the machine. And the machine doesn't want you to see how it works.

But that ends here.

Who "They" Are and Why They Play a Different Game

Let's be clear: "They" are not some shadowy cabal hiding behind curtains. They are lawyers who help multinational corporations avoid taxes in five countries simultaneously. They are accountants who build cash flow structures across entities and decades. They are politicians who quietly own real estate through trusts while passing tax laws "for the people." They are bankers who provide tailored financial products to their elite clients while selling retail debt to everyone else.

They are the financial elite—not just rich in money, but in access. They know how to move capital without triggering taxes. How to own nothing while controlling everything. How to use policy, credit, and law-like tools in a black bag of wealth-building tactics.

And what makes them powerful isn't just money—it's that they play a completely different game than you do.

While you're applying for a mortgage, they're using debt to generate tax-free liquidity through a private line of credit backed by appreciating stock.

While you're building a retirement account that penalizes you for early access, they're investing in pre-IPO tech companies and cash-flowing private deals that never hit public markets.

While you're budgeting groceries and chasing credit scores, they're working through family offices with dedicated in-house legal, tax, and banking teams who make sure they never pay more than 3% in taxes—if that.

What separates them from you isn't just capital. It's a framework. It's how they see money. How they navigate the rules. How they build systems while everyone else follows instructions.

They don't react to the system. They design around it.

They've chosen to play a different game. A game where:

- Money is mobile
- Risk is managed through entities
- Ownership is obscured by the structure
- Liquidity is sourced through credit, not labor
- Legacy is protected, not hoped for

That game has been hidden from you. Until now.

How This Book Will Shift Your Financial Trajectory

This book is not about budgeting. It's not about frugality. It won't scold you for buying coffee or tell you to clip coupons. That's consumer finance. This book is about elite finance—the kind that never makes it into a public podcast or TV interview because it's not meant for mass consumption.

What this book will show you is how the truly wealthy think, operate, and build financial ecosystems that outlast them. More importantly, it will show you how to start using these same principles even if you're not yet wealthy.

You will learn how the wealthy:

- Protect their assets from lawsuits, taxation, and seizure
- Minimize or eliminate taxes through legal and structural means
- Use debt as a strategic financial instrument—not a burden
- Create income streams that are hidden, untaxed, and unearned
- Use layered entities and trusts to shield wealth and remain invisible
- Build legacies that survive governments, market crashes, and generational decline

And you'll learn how to start now.

Because this information isn't just for billionaires. It's for anyone ready to stop being used by the system—and start using it.

Each chapter will unpack a critical component of the hidden wealth ecosystem. You'll see the structures. You'll understand the logic. And you'll be shown exactly where to begin, even with limited capital.

You don't need millions to think like the elite. You need leverage. You need structure. You need to replace assumptions with strategy.

The goal isn't to make you a billionaire. The goal is to make you **sovereign**—free from dependence on any one source of income, employer, or government policy. To give you tools for control, privacy, and resilience in a world where exposure is risky and ignorance is expensive.

Once you see the code behind the game, you can't unsee it. The rules shift. The pressure lifts. And you finally stop playing defense.

This book is not just a financial manual. It's a blueprint for exit. An invitation to stop walking the path designed for you—and start building your own.

You don't have to play small. You just have to play smarter.

This is your financial awakening.

Chapter 1 – The Two Financial Systems: One for Them, One for You

The Illusion of Fairness

The financial system is presented to you as a meritocracy—a level playing field where intelligence, hard work, and discipline are enough to guarantee success. Politicians, teachers, bankers, and financial media figures all push the same comforting lie: "Work hard, play by the rules, and you'll be rewarded."

It's a message embedded in culture, curriculum, and career advice. It's repeated so often and so early in life that it becomes invisible. Most people never stop to question it. They internalize the idea that financial outcomes are a direct reflection of personal virtue. If you're rich, you must have earned it. If you're struggling, you must have failed.

But this belief system is not just false—it's a control mechanism.

Because the truth is, the game was never fair. The financial system is not neutral. It doesn't reward effort equally. It doesn't punish failure evenly. It's engineered to appear just equitable enough to avoid mass dissent while remaining deeply imbalanced in practice. The illusion of fairness is the cornerstone of obedience. Without it, people would revolt.

Consider taxation. The average W-2 employee sees their paycheck drained before it even reaches their bank account. Federal income tax, Social Security, Medicare, state tax—all removed automatically. They have no flexibility, no say in the matter.

Now look at the wealthy. Their income doesn't come as wages—it comes as capital gains, dividends, trust disbursements, and loans backed by appreciating assets. These forms of income are either taxed at a lower rate, deferred indefinitely, or excluded from taxation altogether. They used depreciation schedules, carried interest rules, 1031 exchanges, and charitable write-offs. It's not that they pay less illegally—it's that the structure of their income means they don't have to pay like you do.

This isn't just about rates—it's about categories. You are taxed on earned income, which the system considers the most "taxable" form of revenue. The rich avoid earned income altogether. They live off borrowed money, tax-advantaged cash flow, and returns on capital.

Now look at education. You were likely taught how to be employable, not powerful. Schools teach obedience, not leverage. Most students emerge with no understanding of tax law, debt strategy, or asset protection—but they can recite historical dates and take standardized tests. Meanwhile, children of the elite are taught how to think in ownership, how to use credit as a tool, how to protect assets behind legal structures, and how to manage advisors, not just themselves.

They are taught strategy. You were taught compliance.

It doesn't stop there. Look at the legal system. If a small business owner forgets to pay quarterly taxes, they may be hit with interest, penalties, and possibly legal action. A multinational corporation underreports by millions? They negotiate with the IRS behind closed doors and settle for cents on the dollar—without admitting guilt, without consequences, and often with government incentives still intact.

Look at banking. If you overdraft your checking account, you're hit with fees. If a billionaire needs liquidity, their banker issues a seven-figure loan within hours, secured by art or equity. They never have to sell. They never have to explain. They never have to ask for permission.

And when it comes to investment access, you're handed retail mutual funds and basic ETFs with fees and limited upside. Meanwhile, private equity firms, hedge funds, venture capital syndicates, and offshore opportunity zones are quietly offered to those with connections and the minimum buy-ins—often hundreds of thousands of dollars.

Even mistakes are handled differently. Do you fail in business? You may be bankrupted, your credit ruined. Do they fail in business? They restructure through an entity, raise fresh capital, and write off the loss as a tax benefit.

This is not an economy. It's a hierarchy. And once you see that, you stop blaming yourself for falling behind and start asking a more powerful question: What game are they playing—and how do I start playing it too?

How the Wealthy Bypass the Rules You Follow

The rules you follow were never designed to help you win. They were designed to keep you in line. Save for retirement. Budget responsibly. Avoid debt. Work hard. Be grateful. That's the financial advice you're fed.

But the wealthy don't follow those rules. They navigate around them—and not by breaking them, but by understanding them at a level most people never reach. They don't need loopholes. The entire structure of their financial life is a loophole.

You were told to stash money in an IRA and hope the market behaves for the next 40 years. They establish tax-advantaged trusts and foundations that can grow capital in perpetuity, passing down wealth through generations without triggering estate taxes.

You were told to pay down your mortgage. They buy income-producing real estate, let tenants service the debt, and borrow against the appreciated equity to access cash without selling—and therefore without creating a taxable event. It's infinite leverage.

You were told to avoid debt. They seek it out—on purpose. But it's not consumer debt—it's structured debt, backed by appreciating or cash-flowing assets. It's private credit. It's insurance-backed lending. It's margin from investment portfolios. This debt is cheaper than selling assets, and it's invisible to the tax code.

They don't "cheat" the system. They opt out of the default.

This happens through structure. Even a basic LLC can provide tax flexibility, asset protection, and separation between personal and business risk. But the elite don't stop at LLCs. They use:

- **Holding companies** to own and obscure asset chains
- **Family Limited Partnerships** to reduce taxable estate size
- **Foreign trusts** to protect assets from domestic legal threats
- **Private foundations** to maintain philanthropic control and receive tax benefits
- **S-Corps and C-Corps** for income splitting and fringe benefit optimization

Each layer adds flexibility, control, and invisibility.

Then there's leverage. The rich rarely use their own money when they don't have to. They collateralize everything—from brokerage accounts to collectibles to intellectual property. They borrow at low interest to invest in high-return assets, effectively multiplying their money without giving up ownership or triggering capital gains.

Access is another invisible barrier. Most of the financial tools available to the public are designed for safety, not growth. Meanwhile, elite investors access pre-IPO shares, direct lending deals, special-purpose vehicles, and real estate projects that never hit the open market. They don't compete—they're invited.

But these invitations aren't about luck. They're about structure. You become investible when you show that you understand how to manage risk like an institution—not a consumer. You're trusted when you operate through entities, come with legal teams, and use capital strategically. This is a world built on alignment, credibility, and network—not income.

The most insidious part? Every rule you've been told is necessary—saving in retirement accounts, avoiding leverage, focusing on salary—is a form of control.

And every limitation has a hidden door. Not because the rich are lawless, but because they understand that laws are interpreted through structure.

The wealthy don't follow a different set of laws. They follow a different logic.

They understand how to remove themselves from the line of financial fire—how to shield income, own nothing, control everything, and pass assets down untouched. They play on a different field, with different equipment, and different stakes.

And once you see that, the next move is clear: it's time to stop following rules written for someone else—and start building your system.

Information Asymmetry: The Rich Have Access You Don't

Information is currency—and the wealthy operate with an entirely different currency system than you do.

It's not just that they get better advice. They get a different type of advice altogether—advice tailored to leverage, protection, scalability, and legacy. Advice that isn't public, advertised, or even accessible without wealth, connections, or both. There are two separate financial languages spoken in the world—one for the masses, and one for those who own capital.

Walk into your local bank and ask what they can do for you. You'll be offered a checking account, maybe a savings account with 0.01% interest, a secured credit card if your credit score is low, and a few generic mutual fund options. This is retail finance—mass-produced, heavily regulated, and intentionally simple. It's designed for obedience, not optimization.

Now walk into a private client office or family wealth division. The conversation changes entirely. You'll hear about:

- Structured notes and bespoke debt instruments
- Multi-currency lending across international jurisdictions

- Strategic philanthropy to reduce estate tax liability
- Private equity deals that never hit public markets
- Asset protection trusts located in secrecy jurisdictions
- Multi-entity strategies to split income and reduce exposure

These conversations aren't happening on YouTube or in financial literacy podcasts. They're happening behind closed doors—in estate planning meetings, in legal briefings, in quiet power-lunches at private clubs. And they're only happening for people who already have significant assets to protect—or the foresight to act like they do.

It's not just banking. It's everywhere. Your tax preparer probably files basic returns, focuses on compliance, and works from standardized software. The wealthy don't use tax preparers—they use tax strategists. Entire legal teams coordinate their income structures across multiple states or even countries, using every clause in the tax code to defer, offset, or entirely avoid taxation. Their returns are not simple—they're engineered.

The difference is not intelligence. It's access. There is an entire **shadow curriculum** of financial knowledge that is never taught unless you're in the right circles. Private investor networks. Closed-door conferences. Wealth retreats. Multi-generational estate seminars. Inside these rooms, what's discussed isn't budgeting or retirement—it's asset flow, governance, control, and generational permanence.

The public is deliberately kept out of these rooms. You don't just walk in with a few thousand dollars and curiosity. You need capital. You need legal structures in place. You need vetted relationships. And most importantly—you need the language. Because these aren't conversations about income. They're about infrastructure.

Meanwhile, the information fed to the public is designed for containment. Turn on financial TV or scroll through personal finance TikTok. What are you told?

- Cancel your subscriptions
- Save 10%
- Use a high-yield savings account
- Avoid debt at all costs
- Buy and hold index funds
- Budget everything

It's surface-level content created to keep you compliant. Not because it's all wrong—but because it's insufficient. These tips are like giving someone a lifejacket in a tsunami and saying, "Good luck."

Why is this the default advice? Because the content you're exposed to is bought and paid for. Financial influencers are often sponsored by the very companies that profit from your underperformance. Banks. Credit card issuers. Mutual fund companies. Insurance brokers. They pay to keep the conversation simple—because complexity would cost them.

If you understood what was possible—what tools were available—you'd stop using their products. You'd stop being profitable to them.

The elite operate on a different frequency. They understand how to structure deals, how to shelter cash flow, how to navigate international jurisdictions, how to shield ownership, and how to generate returns instead of wages. They understand the legal, financial, and tax systems because they're not guessing—they're advised by people who help billionaires sleep at night.

They aren't chasing budget hacks. They're creating arbitrage—legal, financial, geographic, and generational.

And here's the kicker: most of the information you need is technically public. But it's buried. It's obscured by complexity. It's written in a different dialect. And unless you're taught how to read it—how to see the architecture behind the numbers—it may as well be invisible.

But once you see it, once you recognize that this is not about IQ but about infrastructure, the playing field changes. What once looked like a mountain becomes a map. And once you hold the map, you stop walking in circles—and start designing your path out.

The Real Purpose of Financial Education (Hint: It's Not for You)

You were taught to view money through a lens of fear and scarcity.

You were taught that debt is bad. That risk is dangerous. That working for a steady paycheck is the responsible thing to do. You were taught to pursue "stability" at the cost of freedom. To simplify. To save. To obey.

But who designed that curriculum? And why?

Public financial education isn't about empowerment. It's about control. It's a well-polished obedience training program that produces tax-paying workers who follow instructions, don't ask questions, and hand their savings over to institutions that profit from managing it.

In school, you weren't taught:

- How the tax code works
- How to structure a business for liability protection
- How to read a balance sheet
- How to use debt to acquire appreciating assets
- How to separate ownership from control
- How to evaluate or structure private investment deals
- How to legally reduce your tax exposure

Instead, you were taught algebra and how to fill out a job application.

That's not a coincidence. It's by design. Because a financially literate population is a threat to centralized control.

If you understood trusts, you'd bypass probate courts.
If you understood corporate structure, you'd protect your income and assets.
If you understood leverage, you'd stop trading time for money.
If you understood the tax code, you'd keep more of what you earned.
If you understood how power works, you'd stop asking for permission.

But you were never supposed to understand those things. You were supposed to be manageable. Predictable. Contained. A productive participant in an economic system that rewards obedience, not ownership.

Meanwhile, look at how the children of the elite are educated about money. They aren't told to "save 10%" or to get a good job. They're taught how to:

- Use trusts to pass on assets tax-free
- Assign voting vs. non-voting equity for control without liability
- Use foundations for legacy and tax efficiency
- Utilize private banking for unregulated lending options
- Avoid lawsuits through corporate layering and anonymity

They are taught not to obey systems—but to own and operate them.

The financial education that most people receive is a mask. A set of behavioral expectations dressed up as wisdom. It teaches you just enough to function—and not enough to win. It produces lifetime consumers, lifetime taxpayers, and lifetime dependents.

And here's the truth: you don't need permission to leave that system. You just need access to the real education. And that begins with understanding what this book is giving you: not tricks, not hacks, but language, logic, and leverage.

You are not broken. You are not stupid. You were simply handed a script that was never written with your freedom in mind.

But now, the script has changed. This book exists to give you the playbook they never wanted you to see. The one that's used in law offices, boardrooms, family offices, and legacy institutions. It's not just about money. It's about architecture—about how wealth is built, protected, and made invisible.

You may not have been born into this knowledge. But you have access to it now.

And once you possess it, nothing is ever the same.

Chapter 2 – Hidden Entities: How the Rich Protect Assets You'll Never See

Shell Corporations, Trusts, and Offshore Accounts

When most people think of wealth, they envision simplicity: a checking account, a 401(k), and a home in their name. To them, owning things outright is the goal—full ownership equals control. But to the ultra-wealthy, this mindset is backward. Owning assets in your name isn't power—it's exposure. It's vulnerability. It's an invitation to lawsuits, taxes, and scrutiny. The truly rich don't own their wealth—they control it through layers of legal protection.

This is why their assets are not held in their names. They are held by **entities**: shell corporations, trusts, and offshore accounts. These aren't shady loopholes or illegal tactics. They are fully legal—because they were designed by the very same lawyers, lobbyists, and lawmakers who serve the elite. These structures form a financial firewall between the individual and their assets, and they are used not only to protect wealth, but to hide it, grow it, and transfer it discreetly across generations and borders.

Shell corporations are often misunderstood. They're not inherently illegal or nefarious—they're legal entities that exist primarily on paper. They have no employees, no physical office, and often no business operations of their own. Their true value lies in what they hold. A shell company might own a luxury condo in Manhattan, a yacht docked in Monaco, a stake in a startup, or intellectual property rights worth millions.

Why use a shell? Because it creates **legal distance** between the asset and the person who benefits from it. If someone sues you, they can't touch what you don't own. If your name isn't on the title, you're harder to target. If regulators come knocking, the trail leads to a holding company, not your personal bank account. Shells aren't illegal—they're invisible shields used by everyone from Fortune 500 CEOs to entertainment moguls to tech founders.

Then come **trusts**, arguably the most powerful and versatile wealth vehicle in the playbook. A trust is a legal arrangement where one party (the trustee) holds assets on behalf of another (the beneficiary), according to terms set by a third (the grantor). On paper, it's simple. In practice, it's genius.

Trusts can be **revocable**, meaning the terms can be changed, or **irrevocable**, meaning they cannot. They can be set up domestically or internationally. They can be rigid or highly flexible. But their primary value is this: they separate **ownership from control**. If you don't technically own the asset, creditors can't reach it. Neither can divorce courts, tax authorities, or nosy journalists.

With the right legal language, you can dictate exactly how your wealth will be used, who benefits when distributions occur, and under what conditions. You can ensure your heirs don't squander your fortune. You can bypass probate and estate taxes. You can maintain absolute privacy while still influencing every move.

Trusts are also a cornerstone of dynasty planning. With **generation-skipping trusts**, wealth can pass down multiple generations without triggering new layers of taxation. With **spendthrift clauses**, beneficiaries can't recklessly blow their inheritance. With **discretionary trusts**, distributions can be made based on your values, not just your bloodline.

And then there are **offshore accounts**—the most controversial and misunderstood asset protection tools of all.

Forget the movie clichés. Offshore accounts aren't about hiding gold bars in a Swiss vault. They are strategic instruments used by multinational corporations, hedge funds, and ultra-high-net-worth families to gain jurisdictional advantage, currency flexibility, and legal insulation.

Countries like **the Cayman Islands, Belize, Nevis, Switzerland, and Singapore** have built entire financial ecosystems around attracting foreign capital. These jurisdictions offer:

- **Strong banking secrecy** laws
- **Flexible trust structures**
- **Low or zero tax rates**
- **Political and economic stability**
- **Favorable legal frameworks** for asset protection

Opening an offshore account isn't illegal. Hiding it and failing to report it might be—but that's not what the wealthy do. They don't hide their money illegally. They make it difficult to trace legally. Funds are held by foreign trusts, which are controlled by offshore LLCs, which in turn are directed by nominee directors. If you wanted to follow the trail, you'd run into a wall of red tape, foreign languages, and sealed documents.

These entities aren't about breaking the law—they're about bending the game in your favor. They create layers. Each layer adds complexity, each layer adds time, and each layer increases the cost of litigation, taxation, and asset seizure. Most lawsuits never make it past layer one. Most creditors give up before they even know what to look for.

Used together, these tools form a defensive fortress. Picture it like this:

- A U.S. irrevocable trust owns a Nevis LLC
- That LLC owns a Swiss bank account and several Delaware corporations
- Those corporations hold real estate, businesses, brokerage accounts, and IP assets
- The trust has a spendthrift clause, a flight clause, and a foreign trustee
- The actual family members? Nowhere on record

This is how the game is played. This is how wealth is structured not just to grow, but to disappear from public view. Not hidden—but **invisible by design**.

The Invisible Family Office

Behind every truly powerful fortune—beyond the headlines, beyond the balance sheets—there is a quiet machine running everything. That machine is the **family office**.

At first glance, the term sounds unremarkable. You might imagine a small team of accountants managing a family's finances. But in reality, a family office is a private financial institution, often structured as its legal entity, that handles everything: investments, legal structuring, tax minimization, risk management, philanthropy, estate planning, and often even security, travel, and education for the family.

The wealthy don't just have "a financial advisor." They have a custom-built command center.

There are two main types:

- **Single-Family Offices (SFOs)**: Created for one ultra-wealthy family, typically with $100M+ in investable assets

- **Multi-Family Offices (MFOs)**: Firms that serve several wealthy families under one platform

But don't be fooled. Even a multi-family office is light-years ahead of any retail wealth service. These firms don't sell products—they **build systems**.

A typical family office will coordinate:

- Complex **tax strategy** across multiple states or countries
- **Private equity and venture capital** allocations
- **Direct real estate deals** outside the public market

- **Estate planning** with trusts, foundations, and asset freeze techniques

- **Philanthropy** via donor-advised funds and private foundations

- **Legal defense layers** in case of litigation or media scrutiny

- **Generational governance structures** to preserve control over time

A family office is, essentially, a **private bank, law firm, hedge fund, and strategy center** rolled into one discreet operation. The name of the game is control without exposure.

Most of the time, you'll never know who's behind the money. The name on the deal is a holding company. The contract is signed by a fiduciary. The address is a P.O. box or law office. The real power stays behind the curtain.

Why do the wealthy build family offices? Because centralized control is safer than delegation to institutions. Banks can collapse. Financial advisors can give bad advice. Governments can change laws overnight. A family office provides continuity, adaptability, and privacy.

And family offices don't just manage money—they create access. They co-invest with top-tier private equity firms, buy into elite real estate portfolios, and participate in pre-IPO placements and off-market deals that the average person will never hear about until years later—when the returns have already been made.

They also engineer permanence. Where most people plan for retirement, family offices plan for dynasties. A family office can be designed:

- **100-year trusts** that prevent asset dissipation

- **Private insurance policies** for tax-free transfers

- **Succession plans** that insulate wealth from divorce, lawsuits, or bad decision-making

- **Voting and non-voting structures** to separate family control from day-to-day business operations

Some family offices even integrate philosophy—they write charters, mission statements, and governance documents that ensure wealth isn't just transferred, but guided. Heirs are educated on stewardship. Some are given access to funds only if they meet certain requirements—like charitable giving, financial literacy, or contributing to family businesses.

The reason you rarely hear about family offices is that they are built to be invisible. They are the **back office of global empires**, the **power structures behind power**, and the **infrastructure of financial sovereignty**.

You see the yacht. You don't see the web of legal entities that own it.

You read about the billionaire. You don't see the five-generation plan his family office is executing behind the scenes.

But make no mistake: family offices are not rare. There are thousands operating today—from Wall Street dynasties to Silicon Valley heirs to foreign aristocracies. And their purpose isn't to manage money—it's to **control it, protect it, and preserve it without ever putting it at risk**.

This is how real wealth moves. Quietly. Legally. Invisibly. And unless you're inside that world, you never even know it's there.

Why the Elite Avoid Personal Ownership

Ownership equals liability. That's the fundamental equation understood by the elite—and ignored by the masses. It's a rule not taught in school, but one that governs the entire strategy of those who operate above the surface-level financial game.

To the average person, owning a home, car, business, or intellectual property in their name is a sign of success. It's how they measure achievement. But to the wealthy, direct ownership is a liability magnet. It ties you to risk. It exposes you to lawsuits. It signals to the system exactly where your wealth lives. And worst of all, it limits your ability to maneuver strategically.

When your name is on the deed, the contract, or the asset, you are the target. Any legal action—divorce, lawsuit, creditor claim, tax audit—comes straight to you. There's no insulation, no buffer, no firewall. That's why the elite go to great lengths to **control everything but own nothing**.

The difference may sound subtle, but it's the bedrock of asset protection. Ownership can be taken. Control can be engineered to be untouchable.

Take real estate. The average homeowner owns their house in their name. That means if they're sued—even in an unrelated matter—that home is fair game. The wealthy? They hold real estate in **LLCs** or **land trusts**, often nested within more complex entities. If a judgment is passed against them, the house isn't technically theirs—it's an asset of a company, which itself may be owned by a trust or offshore entity. That house might be leased to them by their structure.

The same goes for businesses. Most people operate a business as a sole proprietor or simple LLC, exposing their assets to risk. The elite use **holding companies** to own the business, **management companies** to operate it, and **trusts or offshore foundations** to own the holding company. That means if the business is sued or goes bankrupt, their wealth is unaffected—and often, even the true ownership of the business is hard to prove.

Vehicles, yachts, aircraft? These are not registered under the person's name. They're held by corporations and leased for personal use. In the event of a crash, incident, or lawsuit, liability falls on the entity—not the individual.

Even **intellectual property**, such as music catalogs, trademarks, patents, and proprietary content, is often assigned to **intellectual property holding companies**. Those companies then license the IP back to the operating business or third parties—creating tax-efficient royalty streams and legal protection in one move.

Why does this matter? Because **every layer of ownership removed is a layer of risk removed**.

Here's the hidden power of avoiding personal ownership:

- **Reduced tax visibility**: Many tax obligations are triggered at the personal level. If an entity earns the income, distributes it strategically, or reinvests, personal tax events can be deferred or avoided entirely.

- **Lawsuit protection**: Personal assets are vulnerable to litigation. Controlled assets—owned by properly structured entities—are not.

- **Divorce protection**: Assets that aren't technically owned by you aren't subject to division in divorce proceedings—assuming proper structuring and timing.

- **Estate planning**: If you don't own it, there's nothing to pass through probate. Instead, assets pass through trusts, foundations, or offshore arrangements—bypassing estate taxes and government interference.

Perhaps most importantly, avoiding personal ownership enhances **strategic flexibility**. Assets held in your name are locked. Selling them triggers taxes. Moving them is regulated. However, assets held by entities can be restructured, leveraged, or liquidated with far more control.

This is how billionaires walk away from personal bankruptcies untouched. Their wealth isn't in their name—it's in structures. They might default on a personal loan or lose a lawsuit, but the jets still fly, the real estate portfolio keeps cash flowing, and the trust fund keeps growing—because their exposure was carefully minimized from the beginning.

The average person fears losing their assets. The elite design a life where there's **nothing personal to take** in the first place.

That's the difference between **legal ownership** and **functional control**. And in the world of real wealth, control wins—every time.

Secrets of Holding Companies and Asset Layers

Imagine a fortress—not made of stone but of paper, law, and structure. That's the architecture of wealth protection. At the heart of that architecture is the **holding company**—a quiet powerhouse that enables the elite to isolate, protect, and grow their assets while remaining nearly invisible.

A **holding company** is a business entity that doesn't operate a business in the traditional sense. It doesn't sell goods or services. Instead, it owns the things that do. It may hold subsidiaries, real estate, stocks, intellectual property, private equity, or other operating businesses. Its job is simple: **consolidate ownership while distributing risk**.

Let's break it down with a real-world example.

Imagine a wealthy investor owns:

- Three apartment buildings
- A media company
- A digital product business
- A luxury yacht
- A private art collection

The average person might hold these in their name or be scattered across simple LLCs. But the elite go several steps further.

Each apartment building is owned by its own **LLC**—one building, one company. This protects the other buildings from liabilities if a tenant sues over an injury or a fire. The media company is also in a separate LLC, and the digital business in another. The yacht is held by a **maritime corporation**, registered in a favorable jurisdiction. The art is owned by an **art trust**, and managed by a private foundation.

All of these entities are **owned** by a single **holding company**—a parent entity that holds equity in each child company. That holding company, in turn, is owned by a **trust**, which may be managed by a **family office** or offshore trustee. Now try tracing ownership. Good luck.

This is called **layering**. It serves three critical purposes:

1. **Asset isolation**: Every asset is legally firewalled. A lawsuit, tax issue, or business failure in one area doesn't contaminate the others.

2. **Legal invisibility**: On paper, no individual owns anything directly. Ownership is diluted through trusts, entities, and management agreements.

3. **Strategic flexibility**: Each entity can have its tax structure, location, income flow, and function—maximizing efficiency.

Let's go deeper.

A holding company might be set up in **Delaware**, which offers strong legal protections and minimal reporting requirements. Its subsidiaries could be registered in **Nevada** for privacy, **Florida** for favorable trust laws, or **Ireland** for international tax treaties. The holding company can lend money to its subsidiaries, purchase assets across borders, and spin-off divisions for tax or investment purposes.

Want to raise capital? Sell non-voting shares in one subsidiary while retaining full control via the holding company. Want to reduce taxes? Use **inter-company billing**, **royalty transfers**, or **management fees** to shift income across entities and reduce net taxable income in high-tax jurisdictions.

This level of planning isn't done on TurboTax. It's executed by **teams**: tax strategists, corporate attorneys, international law firms, and asset managers. Every dollar moves intentionally. Every contract has layers. Every signature protects someone from liability.

Here's another trick: **staggered ownership**. Let's say your Delaware holding company owns 80% of a media company. The remaining 20% is held by a private foundation you also control. The media company pays dividends. Those dividends go to both entities—but the foundation's share is **tax-exempt**. That's 20% of the profits, tax-free, redirected toward charitable goals or legacy planning.

Or consider **double layering**: A U.S. trust owns a Cayman Island foundation, which owns a Luxembourg holding company, which in turn owns a series of Delaware LLCs. Why so complex? Because complexity is defense. It slows down lawsuits, obscures asset maps, and deters predatory action.

To the average observer, it may seem excessive. But that's because most people play financial checkers. The elite play **multi-board chess**.

And these layers don't just protect assets—they create leverage. You can pledge one subsidiary's assets as collateral while shielding the rest. You can restructure ownership to bring in partners without relinquishing control. You can consolidate revenue while separating liability. And you can exit strategically—selling off pieces of your empire without revealing the whole.

The beauty of holding companies and layered asset structures is that they **compound benefits**: tax savings, privacy, legal protection, investment access, and control. They are not shortcuts. They are architectural advantages that shift the entire game.

This is why the wealthy don't fear volatility, lawsuits, or even death. Their wealth doesn't live in their wallet—it lives in a matrix of structures designed to endure across generations.

If your assets live in your name, they're a target. If they live in layers, they're protected.

This is the power of structure. This is why the rich appear untouchable.

And now that you've seen what lies behind the curtain, you can begin to design your layers—not just to protect what you earn, but to build something that lasts. In the next chapter, you'll see how they use the tax system not to pay their share—but to **write off entire empires**.

Chapter 3 – The Art of Tax Disappearance: Legal Evasion vs. Smart Avoidance

Why the Ultra-Wealthy Pay Less (or Nothing)

The ultra-wealthy do not approach taxes the way ordinary people do—and that's not because they cheat. It's because they **architect** their financial lives differently from the ground up. While the average taxpayer is busy gathering receipts to squeeze out a few deductions each April, the rich are playing an entirely different game—a game in which taxes are not the cost of participation, but an obstacle to be navigated or neutralized.

At the core of this strategy is a simple shift in perspective: **income is a choice**. Most people think of income as something that just "happens"—you work, you earn, and you pay. However the wealthy understand that income can be **transformed, deferred, reclassified**, or **avoided altogether** through legal strategy and structural design.

Let's start with the basic income order. The average person earns a paycheck, pays taxes immediately, and lives on what's left. But the wealthy do the opposite: they **earn through entities, spend through structures**, and **recognize income last, if at all**. The result? Lower reported income. Less exposure. More retained capital.

Consider a wealthy investor with a $20 million real estate portfolio. She doesn't "sell" her properties to realize a gain and get taxed. Instead, she **borrows against her equity**—say, a $5 million tax-free loan—secured by appreciating assets. That loan is **not taxable** because it isn't income. Yet it provides immediate liquidity. She uses that loan to fund her lifestyle, invest in new deals, or lend it out privately for 10–12% returns. Meanwhile, real estate continues to appreciate and generate rent. Her tax return? Almost nothing.

This same principle applies to **stocks and equity**. Jeff Bezos and Elon Musk didn't become rich by taking massive salaries. They own appreciating assets and

borrow against them, often at extremely low interest rates thanks to private bank relationships. The result: ultra-low income, minimal taxes, and compounding wealth.

The tax code isn't a punishment mechanism—it's an **incentive system**. It rewards specific behaviors that governments want to encourage: real estate development, job creation, infrastructure investment, renewable energy, and philanthropy. The wealthy don't break the law—they follow it better than anyone else. Their advisors don't just "do taxes." They **engineer outcomes**.

Here are just a few of the tools the ultra-wealthy use:

- **Depreciation**: They write off the "wear and tear" on buildings, aircraft, and vehicles—even when these assets are appreciated.
- **1031 Exchanges**: They swap one property for another, deferring taxes indefinitely.
- **Installment Sales**: They sell an asset and receive payments over time, reducing the taxable gain each year.
- **Capital Loss Harvesting**: They sell losing assets to offset winning ones.

Family Entities: They shift income to children or trusts in lower tax brackets.

- **Life Insurance**: They grow wealth tax-deferred and borrow against it tax-free.

Perhaps the most important advantage? **Timing control**. When you can choose when and how you recognize income, you control the tax impact. You can align gains with losses. You can postpone income to a low-bracket year. You can convert income into long-term capital gains or qualified dividends. You can defer—sometimes forever.

This is why billionaires often pay less in taxes than their employees. Not because they are evading taxes, but because they've **exited the default system**. They don't operate as individuals—they operate as **ecosystems**, where income doesn't pass through a single channel but is **distributed, sheltered, and transformed** through a network of entities.

And what about death? The average person's estate is taxed, probated, and reduced. The ultra-wealthy structure their assets inside **dynasty trusts, grantor-retained annuity trusts (GRATs)**, and **intentionally defective grantor trusts (IDGTs)**—vehicles that can **transfer hundreds of millions** without triggering gift or estate taxes.

Even the timing of death can be optimized financially. Upon death, an asset's cost basis is "stepped up" to its market value, eliminating unrealized capital gains. That's right: hold an asset until you die, and your heirs may owe nothing on decades of appreciation. It's not accidental. It's the ultimate wealth transfer play.

In the end, tax strategy is **not about finding loopholes**. It's about **controlling outcomes**. The ultra-wealthy don't wait for tax season. They plan every move through the lens of tax optimization. And that's why, year after year, while the middle class sends in checks to the IRS, the rich keep multiplying wealth—untouched and often unseen.

Loopholes in Real Estate, Agriculture, and Foundations

Some of the most powerful tax reduction tools available today are hiding in plain sight—baked directly into the tax code and designed to reward specific behaviors. For those who know how to use them, **real estate, agriculture**, and **private foundations** are not just investments or social tools—they are **tax engines**.

Let's begin with **real estate**, long known as the playground of wealthy investors.

The primary weapon in real estate tax strategy is **depreciation**. When you buy a property, the government allows you to write off its value over time—even as the actual value may be going up. It's an accounting fiction with massive implications. A real estate investor might make hundreds of thousands in rental income, but show a loss on paper because of depreciation. No profit = no income tax.

But the real power comes with **cost segregation**. This strategy breaks a property into parts—HVAC systems, lighting, plumbing, fixtures—and allows each component to be depreciated faster. The result? Giant losses in the early years of ownership offset other income—sometimes even income from entirely unrelated businesses.

Add in **bonus depreciation** and **Section 179 expensing**, and entire properties can be written off in the first year. Investors often buy real estate not for the cash flow—but for the tax losses. They then "stack" properties over time, rolling forward unused losses and deferring taxes indefinitely.

But what if you sell? That's where **1031 exchanges** come in. If you sell a property and reinvest the proceeds into another "like-kind" property, you can defer capital gains tax. In practice, this means you can grow an empire of real estate over decades without ever triggering a taxable event. Some investors use 1031s to delay taxes their entire lives—and then pass the portfolio to their heirs, who receive a **stepped-up basis**. The gains vanish. The taxes evaporate.

Now consider **agriculture**, a less flashy but equally powerful tax haven. Farmland comes with its own set of incentives: **conservation deductions**, **property tax relief**, **equipment depreciation**, **subsidies**, and more.

High-net-worth individuals often acquire farmland not to farm, but to **strategically write off income**. By entering into conservation easements—legal agreements to preserve the land—they receive huge charitable deductions, sometimes far beyond what they paid for the land. These deductions can offset income from businesses, capital gains, and other sources.

Even passive investment in agriculture through **syndications or land funds** can open up depreciation deductions, income tax benefits, and long-term capital gains treatment. In many jurisdictions, agricultural land is exempt from estate tax valuation rules—making it an ideal asset to pass to heirs.

Finally, we arrive at **foundations**—the crown jewel of the wealthy's philanthropic (and tax) playbook.

A **private foundation** is a legal entity that can receive and grow charitable funds. Donating to your foundation provides an immediate tax deduction—up to 30% of your adjusted gross income in cash, or 20% for appreciated stock or assets. But unlike public charities, your foundation is under your control.

You (and your family) can serve as board members, receiving salaries. The foundation can buy or rent offices—from you. It can reimburse travel, host events, or fund research aligned with your interests. As long as the expenses are "related to the charitable purpose," they are permitted.

Better yet, the assets inside the foundation **grow tax-free**. Investments made through the foundation—stocks, real estate, private equity—are not taxed. Only 5% of the assets need to be distributed annually, meaning 95% can sit, grow, and multiply, year after year.

Some wealthy individuals use foundations to **pass on values**, influence public policy, or control intellectual property. Others use them for **reputation laundering**—funding visible causes to maintain social capital while simultaneously optimizing tax exposure.

There's also a hybrid strategy: donate appreciated stock or assets (rather than cash) to the foundation. This avoids capital gains tax and earns a deduction for the full market value. Two tax wins—plus long-term control.

The government created these rules to incentivize certain behaviors. The ultra-wealthy simply took them seriously—and built around them.

They didn't invent depreciation, 1031 exchanges, conservation easements, or foundations. But they mastered them. They turned them from tax "breaks" into

foundations of wealth. These aren't temporary loopholes—they're permanent features of a system designed to reward control, structure, and long-term thinking.

And the good news? With the right education and strategy, **you don't have to be ultra-wealthy to start using them**. You just need to exit the default and start thinking like an insider.

In the next section, we'll look at how the wealthy **pass down assets across generations**—while skipping taxes, court battles, and family chaos.

Dynasty Trusts and Generation-Skipping Strategies

If there's one tactic that separates temporary wealth from enduring dynasties, it's the trust. More specifically, dynasty trusts and generation-skipping strategies—legal tools designed not just to pass down money, but to construct invisible fortresses of wealth that shield capital from taxes, courts, creditors, divorces, and even the unpredictability of future generations. These aren't stopgaps. They are multigenerational vaults engineered for continuity and control.

A **dynasty trust** is a trust built to last—not just for a few decades, but for centuries. In most states, trusts eventually "terminate" due to what's called the rule against perpetuities, which limits how long a trust can exist. But states like South Dakota, Nevada, Alaska, and Delaware have repealed or extended that rule, allowing trusts to exist for hundreds of years—or forever. These states have become havens for legacy planners, offering rock-solid asset protection, privacy, and favorable tax treatment.

Here's how it works: once an individual places assets in a dynasty trust, those assets are no longer considered part of their estate. This means the IRS can't apply estate taxes on them once the grantor dies, nor can future creditors or divorcing spouses lay claim to them. Those assets are instead managed and distributed according to the terms set by the original grantor—terms that may span generations and include specific benchmarks or limitations.

For example, a grantor may stipulate that distributions are only to be made for education, medical emergencies, or business investment. Or that beneficiaries must pass a drug test. Or that no beneficiary can access the principal until the age of 35. The controls are precise, and they're designed not only to preserve wealth—but to preserve discipline. In this way, dynasty trusts serve both financial and behavioral functions: they protect the capital and attempt to shape the character of those who inherit it.

Now let's examine **generation-skipping trusts (GSTs)**. The U.S. tax code normally imposes estate taxes at every generational level: from parents to children, then from children to grandchildren. But GSTs allow the grantor to skip a generation for tax purposes—leaving assets directly to grandchildren or even great-grandchildren. This bypasses a massive layer of taxation and avoids the fragmentation that can occur when each generation splits and spends its inheritance.

Under current tax law, there's a **Generation-Skipping Transfer (GST) tax exemption**—allowing up to a certain amount (currently over $13 million per individual) to be passed to "skip persons" tax-free. Sophisticated planners combine this exemption with valuation discounts, like those applied in family limited partnerships (FLPs), to reduce the appraised value of the assets being transferred. This means they can push even more wealth into GSTs while staying under the exemption threshold.

These strategies don't operate in isolation. The wealthy layer them for maximum impact. Picture this: a high-net-worth individual funds a dynasty trust with business equity or real estate expected to appreciate. The value of the asset is discounted for tax purposes via a FLP. The trust is structured to skip generations using the GST exemption. A trustee—either a bank, lawyer or trusted fiduciary—manages the trust according to pre-set rules. Meanwhile, the beneficiaries can receive income, use assets, and benefit from the trust—without ever technically owning the wealth.

This structure achieves several goals at once:

- Removes assets from the estate, avoiding estate taxes
- Shields assets from personal lawsuits or business liabilities
- Prevents irresponsible heirs from wasting their inheritance
- Ensures continuity of vision and control, long after the grantor is gone
- Provides income and benefits to multiple generations without dilution

And while the average person is encouraged to write a will or open a 401(k), the elite is thinking in dynastic terms. They don't plan for 20 years—they plan for 200. The legal and financial structures they build are designed to endure wars, recessions, divorces, and new governments. They're not just buying time. They're buying permanence.

Most Americans will never hear a financial advisor utter the words "generation-skipping trust." But the wealthy? It's one of their most important tools. Because they understand that the key to legacy isn't just making money. It's protecting it—forever.

The Role of Charitable Trusts and Nonprofits in Tax Shielding

Philanthropy and tax strategy might seem like contradictory ideas—one is seen as generous and selfless, the other as self-serving and calculated. But in the world of elite finance, they coexist powerfully. Charitable giving isn't just about goodwill. It's about control, influence, and engineering tax-advantaged environments where wealth can thrive quietly and indefinitely. For the ultra-wealthy, charitable structures aren't donations. They're strategy.

Let's start with the **Charitable Remainder Trust (CRT)**. This is a legal entity where a person donates an asset—often appreciated stock or real estate—into the trust. Once the asset is inside, it can be sold without incurring capital gains taxes. The proceeds are then reinvested, and the donor receives a fixed income stream (either a set amount or a percentage of the trust's value) for life or a term of years. When the trust term ends, whatever is left goes to a charity.

This achieves multiple things:

- The donor gets a large **immediate tax deduction**, based on the projected value of the eventual charitable gift.

- They sidestep the capital gains tax they would have paid by selling the assets themselves.

- They still enjoy income from the trust for decades.

- And they enhance their public image by "giving" millions—while still benefiting personally.

Then there's the **Charitable Lead Trust (CLT)**—the mirror image of a CRT. In a CLT, the charity gets the income first, for a set number of years. Then, the remaining assets go back to the donor's family or heirs. The strategy here is to shrink the size of the donor's taxable estate. Let's say a wealthy individual places $10 million into a CLT and directs $500,000 per year to go to charity for 20 years. When the term ends, any remaining growth—say $15 or $20 million—goes to the heirs. And because of the way the trust was structured and valued upfront, the gift might pass free of estate or gift tax.

Now consider the **Donor-Advised Fund (DAF)**—a kind of charitable checking account with almost no oversight. The donor puts money into the fund and gets a full tax deduction that year. But the actual charitable distributions can be made slowly, even decades later. In the meantime, the money grows tax-free. There are no strict deadlines, no required minimum distributions, and virtually no public scrutiny. It's the perfect blend of deduction now, and control later.

DAFs are especially appealing because they require far less capital and regulatory complexity than private foundations. But for the truly wealthy, creating their own **501(c)(3) private foundation** is the ultimate move.

A private foundation offers significant control. It's a legal entity that can:

- Pay salaries to family members
- Lease or purchase real estate
- Host extravagant "charitable" events
- Fund causes aligned with the founder's business or political agenda
- Contract with service providers who happen to be part of the same network or family

In other words, a private foundation can operate as a second family office—with tax exemptions, social credibility, and PR benefits baked in.

And while the IRS requires that foundations distribute at least 5% of their assets each year for charitable purposes, how that money is distributed is often incredibly flexible. For example, a foundation might fund a scholarship in the family's name—while hiring the founder's niece to administer the program. Or it may "support education" by giving grants to think tanks that promote favorable economic policies.

All this while the foundation's assets continue to grow, tax-free, shielded from estate taxes, and removed from the founder's taxable estate.

Another sophisticated tool is the **Pooled Income Fund**, which functions like a CRT but combines donations from multiple donors. It's less common among the ultra-wealthy but useful for donors who want to split the benefits of pooled investing and tax deductions without the hassle of running a foundation.

It's important to understand that these vehicles aren't accidental loopholes. They are embedded in the tax code, placed there to encourage giving—but the wealthy know how to exploit them to their fullest potential. They don't simply give money away. They give it in a way that:

- Shields their estate
- Defers or eliminates taxes
- Generates income
- Enhances legacy and reputation
- Provides long-term influence over educational, political, or cultural institutions

To the public, these moves look generous. But in reality, they often amount to **strategic repositioning** of capital. The family wealth isn't disappearing. It's being shifted into forms that are legally protected, publicly praised, and privately controlled.

Even when the money is eventually spent by the charity, the founder's name remains on the building, the scholarship, or the think tank forever. The result? Tax benefits today. Legacy tomorrow. Influence always.

One more critical point: these charitable tools also act as a **safety valve** during years of unusually high income or major liquidity events. Selling a company? You can shield millions from capital gains taxes by contributing pre-sale shares to a DAF or CRT. Facing a spike in income from carried interest or equity? A large foundation gift can offset the exposure while cementing your image as a socially responsible leader.

This isn't small planning. This is an empire design. And it's happening quietly, legally, and relentlessly—right now.

As we move into the next chapter, you'll learn how debt—something the middle class is taught to fear—is wielded by the wealthy as a **strategic weapon**. If charitable vehicles represent the protective side of wealth strategy, debt represents the offensive line. And in the elite playbook, it's one of the most powerful tools of all.

Chapter 4 – Debt Alchemy: Using Other People's Money Like the Billionaires Do

Why Debt Is Power in the Elite Playbook

To the average person, debt is synonymous with danger. It's a credit card balance racking up interest. It's a student loan looming over decades. It's a mortgage that traps you in a job you hate. Debt, for most people, is a chain—a weight that restricts freedom and increases vulnerability. But for the wealthy, debt is something else entirely. It's a **leverage point**. A tax shield. A method of accelerating opportunity. It is power—when wielded correctly.

This isn't just a philosophical difference. It's structural. The middle class is taught to think of debt in terms of consumption: borrowing to buy things they can't afford today, and paying more over time. The rich use debt for production and preservation. They borrow not to survive—but to grow. To unlock capital without surrendering equity. To control assets without triggering tax bills. To maneuver through markets without being exposed.

Take a look at the most successful business figures in the world. They aren't cashing out their stock to fund their lifestyles. They're **borrowing against it**. Jeff Bezos, Elon Musk, and Larry Ellison—they've all used stock-backed loans instead of selling equity. Why? Because the moment you sell, you create a taxable event. But if you **borrow** against the asset, you retain the ownership and avoid taxes.

Debt becomes a tool of **tax arbitrage**. A billionaire can access $50 million in liquidity via a loan secured by their assets, pay a 2-5% interest rate, and use that money to reinvest, purchase real estate, or fund philanthropic projects—all while the underlying asset continues to appreciate. And that interest? Often deductible. The loan? Not considered income. The tax burden? Nearly zero.

This kind of financial engineering isn't reckless. It's **risk-managed leverage**—underwritten by teams of lawyers, accountants, and bankers who ensure that every structure serves the purpose of preserving control while reducing friction. The debt is structured with flexible terms, long maturities, and multiple exit options. In many cases, the repayment can be indefinitely deferred or covered by the cash flow of the very assets being leveraged.

Compare this with the average person's relationship with debt. They're borrowing at high interest rates, with rigid repayment schedules, against depreciating or non-performing assets. The structure is entirely different. And that's the key: **debt is only dangerous when it's misaligned with purpose**. The rich don't use debt to buy liabilities—they use it to buy or access more assets.

The educational system reinforces this divide. People are taught to fear debt rather than understand it. They're told to become debt-free as a virtue, without ever being shown how **strategic leverage** could unlock access to capital they'll never save in a lifetime.

In the elite playbook, debt is not the enemy. It is the engine. And they don't just tolerate it—they master it.

Leveraging Assets Without Selling Them

If you had a Picasso hanging in your living room, would you sell it every time you needed cash? Of course not. You'd take it to the right institution and **borrow against it**. You'd keep the painting, enjoy its appreciation, and use the funds for whatever you needed—without losing ownership or triggering capital gains. That's exactly how the ultra-wealthy approach all their assets.

Selling is inefficient. It creates tax consequences, public disclosures, and often unnecessary loss of control. But borrowing against assets? That's elegant. That's stealthy. And most importantly, that's untaxed.

The process is surprisingly simple—if you have access. Wealthy individuals can approach private banks or boutique lenders and pledge their stock portfolios, real estate, or even artwork as collateral for a line of credit or term loan. These are known as **asset-backed loans**, and they often come with incredibly favorable terms. In many cases, the interest rate is under 5%, the loan is non-recourse (meaning the borrower isn't personally liable beyond the asset), and the underwriting process is discreet.

Let's say you own $25 million in blue-chip stock. Instead of selling and taking a hit on capital gains, you pledge the shares and borrow $10 million. You now have liquid capital without changing your portfolio or sending a dime to the IRS. Better yet, if the stock appreciates, you still enjoy the upside. You're effectively spending your wealth without reducing it.

Real estate works the same way but with even more flexibility. A billionaire who owns a skyscraper isn't going to sell it to buy another asset—they're going to **refinance** it. They take out a new loan on the property's increased value, pull out millions in tax-free cash, and use that capital for new acquisitions. The property remains in their portfolio, continues to generate rental income, and serves as a perpetual ATM.

The same goes for life insurance. **Permanent life insurance policies** with cash value—such as whole life or indexed universal life—allow policyholders to borrow against the policy at favorable terms. This creates a tax-free income stream in retirement or a liquidity option for investments. The policy itself remains intact and continues to grow, and the death benefit passes to heirs tax-free, often wiping out any outstanding loan balances in the process.

And then there's **private business equity**. Let's say you're the founder of a startup now worth $100 million. Selling shares means not just taxes, but possibly giving up control or affecting public perception. So instead, you use those shares as collateral for a personal loan. Private banks will lend based on projected valuations, future revenue, or even expected acquisition outcomes. Again, the capital flows, but the structure remains untouched.

Even more obscure but powerful is the use of **hard assets** like art, classic cars, and rare collectibles. These are increasingly being accepted as collateral by specialized lenders, especially if they're verified, insured, and stored professionally. The asset stays in a vault; the capital enters your account.

All of this points to a single truth: **leverage is about liquidity without sacrifice**. The rich don't have to choose between owning and spending. They do both—because they understand how to turn assets into cash without liquidating them.

This is also why you'll never see a fire sale in elite circles. When they need cash, they don't sell. They borrow. And they do it through legal, structured, sophisticated lending mechanisms that the average person doesn't even know exist.

More importantly, this borrowing is strategic. It allows them to move quickly in a crisis, seize opportunities in a downturn, or fund expansion without public scrutiny. No SEC filings. No board votes. Just quiet capital flowing where it's needed.

While the middle class budgets and saves, the wealthy **unlock their balance sheet**—moving money silently through a system of credit lines, refinances, and portfolio-backed facilities. It's a different game entirely. One where liquidity, privacy, and growth can all be achieved—without selling a single thing.

And this is only the beginning. In the next sections, we'll explore how the wealthy tap into **exclusive investment deals** that generate returns most people will never see—deals that are often made possible only through the silent, fluid power of strategic debt.

Strategic Credit: Business Lines, Private Banking, and Collateralized Loans

For the average borrower, credit is a standardized product: a mortgage, a credit card, a car loan—products with fixed terms, rigid underwriting, and relatively narrow scopes of use. The wealthy don't settle for products. They negotiate **relationships**. They customize **structures**. And this changes everything.

At the core of elite credit is the **private bank**—an exclusive division within major financial institutions dedicated solely to high-net-worth clients. These banks don't simply offer loans. They create **bespoke financing packages** designed to unlock liquidity without forcing asset sales or tax events. Private bankers become trusted advisors who understand their clients' entire financial picture—portfolio, businesses, assets, liabilities—and tailor credit accordingly.

One of the most common products is the **securities-based line of credit (SBLOC)**. This is a revolving credit facility secured by an investment portfolio, often stocks, bonds, or mutual funds. Instead of selling shares to raise cash, the client borrows against their portfolio's value—sometimes up to 70-85%. Interest rates are low, often prime plus a margin, reflecting the low risk to the lender.

This arrangement offers unparalleled flexibility. If the portfolio declines, margin calls might occur, but private banks typically work discreetly with clients to manage risk without forcing forced sales or public alerts. This invisibility preserves both privacy and portfolio integrity.

Business owners with consistent cash flow can access **asset-based lending (ABL)**. Unlike traditional bank loans that rely on credit scores or income statements, ABL is backed by tangible business assets—accounts receivable, inventory, equipment, or contracts. This form of lending is particularly valuable for companies experiencing rapid growth or cyclical revenue. Interest-only payments and minimal reporting reduce administrative burdens. The funds can be deployed for expansion, acquisitions, payroll, or even personal liquidity.

Beyond traditional assets, specialized lenders provide credit secured by **illiquid holdings**—private equity stakes, venture capital interests, royalties, patents, and trademarks. These lenders, often private funds or boutique finance firms, use proprietary valuation methods to assess collateral value. This broadens the spectrum of wealth that can be leveraged, turning what was once "locked up" into accessible capital.

One of the most sophisticated concepts in this arena is **credit arbitrage**.

Imagine borrowing $10 million at an interest rate of 3% and deploying that capital into an investment yielding 10%. The spread—7%—represents a powerful, largely untaxed profit margin. Even the interest expense might be deductible, further increasing net returns. When structured through appropriate entities, this amplifies returns and accelerates wealth compounding.

The difference between the credit accessible to the wealthy and the public isn't just the interest rate or collateral. It's the **mindset**. The average borrower views credit as a last resort, a burden to be minimized or eliminated. The wealthy see credit as **amplification**—a multipurpose tool to scale investments, optimize taxes, preserve capital, and unlock hidden value.

They maintain multiple lines of credit—often with overlapping collateral—to maximize flexibility and reduce risk. When one facility tightens, another can be tapped. When interest rates rise, they refinance or switch lenders quietly. And unlike public borrowing, these credit arrangements rarely require monthly income verification or rigid repayment schedules.

This ongoing, dynamic credit management is a hallmark of elite financial agility. The ability to access capital on demand, with favorable terms, backed by diverse asset classes, empowers opportunities that are close to most investors.

In short, **strategic credit** is a form of financial leverage reserved for those who understand, manage, and control their wealth as a system—not just a number.

The Difference Between "Good" Debt and "Manipulated" Debt

Most personal finance advice introduces a simple dichotomy: **good debt** versus **bad debt**. Good debt is borrowing that builds assets or income—like a mortgage or student loan. Bad debt funds consumption and loses value—credit cards, auto loans, payday loans. This is helpful for everyday budgeting, but it barely scratches the surface of how the wealthy use debt.

The ultra-wealthy don't just use "good" debt. They **design and manipulate debt** to transform wealth itself. Debt becomes a **legal instrument of**

transformation—turning illiquid capital into usable cash, deferring taxes, shielding assets, and enabling control without relinquishing ownership or triggering transparency.

Consider real estate once more. The average homeowner carries a mortgage and pays it down over decades, building equity slowly while paying interest. The wealthy continually **refinance**, extracting cash from appreciated property to fund new investments or personal use. This recycling of capital, combined with the tax deductibility of mortgage interest and depreciation, turns a residence or commercial building into a **financial engine** rather than just a shelter.

In business, the wealthy avoid taking dividends or salaries that would trigger income tax. Instead, they borrow against their equity stakes in private companies—using loans that don't count as taxable income. This preserves the company's value, avoids tax events, and maintains control. It's a classic example of **income transformation** via debt.

Estate planning also leverages debt in sophisticated ways. Wealthy individuals might lend money to their trusts or heirs at the IRS's prescribed minimum interest rates, often called the **Applicable Federal Rate (AFR)**. This "freeze" strategy locks in the estate's value at today's levels, while the assets within the trust continue to appreciate tax-free. The loan repayment can be deferred or waived later, enabling efficient intergenerational wealth transfer with minimal tax consequences.

Debt manipulation also extends to **capital velocity**. The wealthy don't let cash sit idle; they move it aggressively. They might borrow against one asset to purchase another, then refinance the new asset to pay down the first loan. Meanwhile, both assets appreciate and generate income independently. This **circular flow of capital** creates continuous leverage, compounding wealth exponentially.

Unlike reckless borrowing, this is meticulously planned and backed by teams of tax attorneys, financial advisors, and legal counsel. Every transaction is documented, compliant, and structured to maximize advantage.

Most people associate debt with risk and anxiety. The wealthy associate it with **power and control**—because they know how to use it in alignment with growth, liquidity, and tax efficiency.

When debt is engineered as a tool—not a trap—it becomes a **machine of freedom**. It funds opportunity, amplifies returns, and accelerates wealth creation. It is the ultimate resource, deployed intelligently and deliberately.

As we move forward, you will see how this philosophy extends beyond banks and loans. The wealthy leverage their creditworthiness to gain access to **exclusive investment opportunities** and deals you never heard about. Because in the world of the elite, true wealth isn't just what you own—it's the opportunities you can unlock with the right leverage, the right timing, and the right relationships.

Chapter 5 – The Private Deal Pipeline: Where the Real Wealth Happens

Angel Networks, Syndicates, and Pre-IPO Access

Most people are told that wealth is built by holding a diversified portfolio of public stocks for 30 years. That does preserve capital—but it rarely **creates** generational fortunes. Serious money is forged in the private markets, years before a company rings a stock exchange bell. That's where shares are still cheap, information is asymmetric, and a single small check can turn into life-altering equity. The catch? You need **access**—and access lives inside invitation-only ecosystems.

Angel Networks: the first gate

True angel clubs are not Meetup groups; they're curated circles of founders turned investors, domain experts, and family-office principals. Screening committees pick only a handful of deals each month, and each member quietly wires anywhere from $ 10k to $ 500k into a round that the public won't even know exists. The paperwork is simple—often a SAFE or convertible note that postpones valuation debates—but the upside is enormous: get in at a $5 m cap, ride the Series A re-price to $50 m, watch a Series C push it to $500 m, and you've 100-xed before CNBC utters the ticker symbol.

Membership isn't bought with money alone. You need a **signal**: an exit of your own, deep sector knowledge, or a secure referral from a respected member. The reward is not just deal flow but inside-track intelligence—founder references, diligence notes, side-letter rights, and occasionally advisory shares for helping the company close strategic customers.

Syndicates and SPVs: scale without hassle

AngelList popularized the modern **syndicate**: a lead investor performs due diligence and then opens a deal-specific LLC (an SPV) to back-fill capital from followers. Investors commit $ 1k–$ 250k, pay a small carry (profit share) to the lead, sign documents online, and get a single K-1 at tax time. This structure solves three problems:

1. **Aggregation**—founders see only one line on the cap table.

2. **Leverage**—smaller investors pool into seven-figure checks.

3. **Curation**—the lead's reputation rides on every deal, incentivizing real diligence.

Private syndicates go further. A top operator in, say, cybersecurity might spin up a stealth SPV open only to five Fortune 500 CISOs. In return for their $250k tickets, those CISOs promise pilot contracts. That accelerates the startup's revenue and de-risks the investment before the ink is dry.

Pre-IPO secondaries: The Secret Bazaar

Well before a splashy IPO, there's a vigorous **secondary market** where early employees, founders, and seed investors quietly unload shares. Specialized brokers match them with hedge funds, sovereign wealth funds, and ultra-rich individuals hungry for allocation. Prices are opaque, negotiated deal by deal, and sometimes bundled with **forward contracts** that delay the actual transfer until a liquidity event—circumventing insiders' lock-up restrictions.

Early-stage pre-IPO shares often come with preferred-stock protections (liquidation preference, anti-dilution) that retail IPO buyers never get. Even more valuable are **information rights**: quarterly financials, board decks, and pro-rata entitlements in future rounds. Essentially, you see the movie before the trailer drops.

Building the pipeline

Elite investors don't sit back waiting for email blasts. They stack the odds by:

- **Sitting on advisory boards**—a $25k angel check plus domain expertise earns them 0.5% equity and first-look rights on every new venture spinning out of that founder circle.

- **Hosting founder dinners**—potent deal-flow magnets because entrepreneurs crave capital paired with influence.

- **Funding incubators or scout programs**—small grants to university lab spin-outs or a scout allocation in a top-tier VC fund buys perpetual early access.

- **Leveraging personal brands**—a podcast, newsletter, or Substack with 200k niche readers signals reach; founders court such visibility with friendly terms.

By the time the retail crowd scrambles for IPO allocations at $45 a share, insiders are already discussing which of their **$2-series seed shares** they'll allocate to charity for the tax deduction. That's not luck. It's engineered proximity.

Private Equity and Venture Capital for the Inner Circle

If Wall Street is the public lobby, **private equity (PE) and venture capital (VC)** are the penthouse elevators. They control staggering pools of capital and, more importantly, the **terms** under which that capital is deployed. Money is only part of the attraction; power, governance, and optionality are the real prizes.

How private-equity machines print fortunes

A classic buy-out fund raises $5 bn from pension plans, university endowments, and billionaire family offices. It uses 2 % per-year management fees to keep lights on, but the upside is the **20 % carried interest** on profits. The GP (general partner) buys a sleepy manufacturing firm for $500 m, finances 60 % with cheap debt, slashes redundant divisions, tacks on two complementary acquisitions, and then sells the combined entity to a strategic buyer for $1.5 bn. Leverage magnifies the equity return fourfold; tax law treats carry as long-term capital gains. Limited partners receive double-digit IRRs, and the GP prints hundreds of millions—often reinvested into the next fund.

But the real art lies in **structured downside protection**. Deals are layered with preferred equity, PIK notes (payment-in-kind), and management fee offsets. Even if the company sells for a middling price, the fund may still meet its preferred return hurdles, guaranteeing the GP carry. Public-market investors rarely see such self-serving term sheets; in PE, they're standard.

Access is scarce. Minimum tickets run $5–$10 m, and many funds are **capacity-constrained**—closed to new LPs unless an existing investor drops out. Family offices circumvent this by:

- **Seeding emerging managers**—writing the first $50 m anchor check in exchange for permanent co-invest rights with zero fees.

- **Purchasing secondary LP stakes**—buying out institutions that need liquidity mid-fund, often at a discount.

- **Creating club deals**—several families jointly acquire a target, bypassing fund fees altogether.

Venture capital: asymmetric rockets

VC is PE's high-octane cousin. A $200 m VC fund might make 25 bets, knowing most will fail but one could return the entire fund. To play, you need both capital and **signal**: founders accept term sheets not just for money, but for reputation, network, and future fundraising muscle.

Insiders exploit:

- **Pro-rata rights**—the guaranteed ability to maintain ownership in later rounds, where check sizes balloon.

- **Super pro-rata or "major investor" clauses**—letting them double down ahead of outside money.

- **Side letters** offering board observer seats, information rights, or veto powers over key decisions.

Many VCs spin-off **opportunity funds**—vehicles dedicated to late-stage follow-ons in their winners. Existing LPs get first refusal; outsiders are shut out. Some firms even raise **SPAC sidecars** to take portfolio companies public quickly, capturing underwriting fees and warrants on top of venture returns.

Why control beats yield

Public investors chase quarterly performance. PE and VC players pursue **control options**: board seats, blocking rights, liquidation preferences, and redemption clauses. These rights let them dictate exit timing, pivot strategy, and engineer secondary sales to themselves at favorable valuations (so-called **continuation funds**).

Because these deals are private, pricing is negotiated, not discovered. If macro markets wobble, funds aren't forced sellers—valuations are merely marked-to-model. Volatility becomes muted; the downside is delayed. The upside, however, can still explode when a trophy asset IPOs or is acquired.

For the ultra-wealthy, committing $10 m across three elite funds isn't diversification—it's **positional leverage**. They gain:

- **First-look privileges** on co-investments with no management fee or carry

- **Information arbitrage**—quarterly calls with GPs revealing trends long before they hit Bloomberg terminals

- **Relationship capital**—sitting on boards alongside Fortune 500 CEOs or former secretaries of state

- **Deal recycling**—rolling distributions from one exit into the next fund's first closing, compounding inside a closed loop

In PE and VC, you're not just buying an asset. You're buying a **seat at the creation table**—shaping industries, influencing policy, and capturing value curves before they reach public view. The goal isn't a tidy 8 % yield. It's a 10–

50× step-function gain that rewrites a family balance sheet—or, in some cases, reshapes an entire sector.

How the Rich Buy Cash Flow, Not Jobs

The middle class is conditioned to equate a paycheck with prosperity: trade enough hours and you'll be secure. The wealthy treat that logic as an entry-level stepping-stone. What they covet is **recurring, controllable cash flow**—income that arrives whether they work or sleep, that can be forecasted, insured, or borrowed against. Instead of hunting promotions, they hunt yield curves, rent rolls, royalty agreements, and interest schedules.

Rule #1: Income should survive you

A job ends when you do. A properly structured asset outlives its owner, pays heirs, and can even be pledged as collateral to fund the next purchase. This mindset nudges the wealthy to ask one question before any acquisition: "Will this produce dependable distributions with minimal oversight?" If the answer is yes, appreciation is the icing on the cake.

Portfolio components that print checks

1. **Commercial Real Estate Power Blocks**

    - **Multifamily complexes:** 200-unit apartments throw off quarterly dividends while onsite management handles tenants.

    - **Industrial warehouses:** Long-term leases to logistics firms indexed to inflation—no phone calls about clogged toilets.

    - **Triple-net retail (N):** Tenants pay taxes, insurance, and maintenance; owners collect rent with near-bond-like certainty.

2. **"Boring" Operating Businesses**

    - **HVAC & plumbing firms:** Emergency demand, sticky

service contracts, and recession resilience.

- **Self-storage facilities:** Minimal labor, automated access control, and high delinquency fees that boost yield.

- **Niche SaaS platforms:** 90 %+ gross margins, prepaid annual subscriptions, and near-zero inventory.

- **Dental and vet roll-ups:** Professional practices aggregated under a management company, delivering 20-30 % EBITDA margins.

3. **Private Credit & Debt Funds**

Wealthy families often act as the bank: loaning to developers, manufacturers, or e-commerce sellers at 9-12 % yields, secured by real assets. These loans float above junk-bond rates yet remain senior to equity, offering downside protection without stock-market noise.

4. **Royalty & Licensing Streams**

- **Music catalogs** are purchased at 12-15× annual royalties and then securitized.

- **Energy royalties**—mineral rights that spin-off revenue whenever hydrocarbons or renewables are harvested.

- **Franchise IP** is rented to operators for a percentage of gross sales.

5. **Insurance-Backed Note Programs & Structured Products**

Instruments that pay predictable coupons (5-8 %) while embedding downside buffers through option overlays or insurer guarantees. Not sexy—but it's reliable grease for monthly cash buckets.

Systems, not side-hustles

The rich rarely "manage" these assets day-to-day. They install third-party operators and performance dashboards that track KPIs in real-time. If returns slip, they replace managers—not grind harder themselves. Cash flow buys time; time buys more deals; more deals compound into an empire.

A dollar from a job can't be redeployed until after taxes and consumption. A dollar from an asset can be:

- **Re-invested** into higher-yield projects.
- **Collateralized** for new credit lines.
- **Securitized** and sold, crystallizing years of distributions up front.

This is how families wake up to ACH deposits, not alarm clocks, and why their "work" involves board calls and acquisition memos rather than timesheets.

Why You'll Never Hear About the Best Investments (Until It's Too Late)

Information doesn't trickle downhill by accident; it's throttled on purpose. By the time an opportunity trends on Reddit or makes a CNBC segment, two things are true: insiders have already set their sell orders, and the risk/reward ratio has inverted. **Access asymmetry**—not IQ or hustle—is the decisive edge.

Deal flow lives behind relationship walls.

Ultra-valuable opportunities circulate in concentric layers:

1. **Founder circles & operator dinners** – unannounced seed rounds, convertible notes with MFN clauses.

2. **Angel syndicates** – curated by leads who want only value-added capital.

3. **Family-office co-invest clubs** – seven-figure checks, no management fee, zero carry.

4. **Institutional shadow books** – banks quietly placing $50 M into secondary blocks at negotiated discounts.

Retail investors see announcements after regulatory filings—long after the price has baked in upside.

Why the gatekeeping?

- **Speed:** Trusted allies wire money in a day, no months-long roadshow.
- **Simplicity:** One or two sophisticated parties keep cap tables clean.
- **Reciprocity:** Today's insider lets you into their deal; tomorrow you slot them into yours.
- **Discretion:** A lower media profile reduces legal exposure and competitive copycats.

Mechanics of the early-bird premium

- **Valuation compression:** Pre-seed startups valued at $3 M might IPO at $3 B—a 1,000× step-up unreachable post-Series B.
- **Preferred rights:** Liquidation preferences and anti-dilution protect the downside—a cushion retail never sees.
- **Side letters:** Information rights, pro-rata guarantees, or super-pro-rata carve-outs let insiders double down before momentum rounds.

By contrast, public-facing tranches come with higher prices, fewer rights, and marketing overhead baked into the cost.

The illusion of "open to all"

Crowdfunding portals and Reg A+ offerings claim democratization, yet issuers list there after failing to close insider rounds. Terms are standardized, diligence is minimal, and the upside has been pre-packaged for a fee. In essence, leftovers.

Breaking into the circle

The door isn't locked, but it is guarded by three keys:

1. **Capability Signaling** – Demonstrate value (technical expertise, distribution reach, deal-scout pipeline) before requesting an allocation.

2. **Capital Readiness** – Have dry powder, entity docs, and wiring protocols ready; hot deals close in 48 hours.

3. **Credible Referrals** – One warm intro from a respected insider beats 100 cold emails.

Start small: invest through micro-sponsor SPVs, volunteer diligence for a syndicate, or provide strategic partnerships to startups. Over time, your name surfaces in those private WhatsApp chats where real allocations get parceled out.

Missing the signal costs millions.

- By the time TikTokers pumped "hot" SPACs, PIPE investors had warrants locked in at half the price.

- When crypto launched mainstream ETFs, early seed-round token holders were rotating into real estate.

- As suburban multifamily exploded in 2021 headlines, families that bought land in 2012 were already refinancing tax-free and redeploying.

Access → Opportunity → Wealth → Access (loop). Break in once, and momentum can carry you forward. Stay outside, and you'll fund someone else's exit.

Chapter 6 – Invisible Income Streams: Quiet Money They Don't Talk About

Licensing, Royalties, and Intellectual Property Tricks

Most people wake up and exchange labor for income. The elite wakes up to wire transfers triggered by contracts they signed years ago. Their secret is turning ideas—software code, branding, patents, literary copyrights—into perpetual cash machines. They rarely manufacture, ship, or service anything themselves. Instead, they retain ownership of intellectual property (IP) and rent it to others in ways that are both tax-efficient and discreet.

Start with a straightforward example: a boutique software firm develops a powerful algorithm but never "sells" it. Instead, it grants—say—five-year licenses to Fortune 500 companies at $250,000 per installation plus an annual maintenance fee. The code doesn't leave the vault; the rights are leased. Cash flows. No factory is required. Should the tax authority come knocking, the company may be domiciled in an IP-friendly jurisdiction such as Ireland or Luxembourg, where royalties are lightly taxed or even exempt.

Authors and musicians do this instinctively—royalties from streaming, reprints, or foreign-language editions hit their accounts whether they're on tour or vacation. But wealthy families super-size the concept:

- **Brand licensing** – A legacy clothing label might sell its retail division yet keep trademark ownership. The buyer pays 3–5 % of gross sales back to the family trust every quarter to keep using the name.

- **Patent royalty overrides** – An inventor places patents into an LLC; multinational manufacturers pay per-unit fees. Even if the LLC is sold, an override clause ensures the original owner continues to skim revenue.

- **Content franchises** – A children's series is optioned for toys, theme parks, and streaming. Each format generates separate royalty streams, all funneling back into an offshore holding company that reinvests tax-deferred.

Then comes the **double-dip strategy**: a parent company transfers its IP into a wholly owned subsidiary in a low-tax country. The operating company in a high-tax region then pays deductible royalties to the IP subsidiary, shifting profit out of harm's way. Multinational tech giants have used "Double Irish, Dutch Sandwich" tactics for decades, but scaled-down versions work for smaller enterprises too.

Income character matters as well. Royalty payments often qualify as passive or portfolio income, taxed at lower rates than wages. In several jurisdictions, royalties can even be reclassified as capital gains through partnership structures, cutting the rate further. Pair this with accelerated amortization of intangible assets, and you get "paper losses" that wipe out other taxable income.

Privacy is baked in. A consumer may see a blockbuster film or global beverage but never know the ultimate recipient of licensing fees. Those payments cascade into trusts, foundations, and special-purpose vehicles that reveal nothing on public registers. To outsiders, wealth appears modest; inside the vault, royalty waterfalls gush.

Asset Leasing, Private Lending, and Hidden Passive Income

The wealthy dislike selling because selling means **taxes**. Leasing is an elegant workaround. Any high-value asset—jet engines, CAT scanners, Stradivarius violins—can become a rental unit that spews non-salary income while the owner retains the title.

Real-estate leasing beyond "landlord basics." A family office converts a brownstone into a film-set venue: $15,000 a day, plus overtime. A downtown loft is furnished as executive crash space for Fortune 100 CEOs—leased at five times normal rent via corporate housing platforms. Cash flows arrive as business revenue, offset by depreciation and cost-seg deductions that wipe out taxable profit on paper.

Equipment leasing scales this concept industrially. Imagine buying $8 million in MRI machines. Hospitals hate tying up capital, so they sign ten-year leases with maintenance baked in. The lessor (often an LLC owned by a trust) finances the purchase with low-interest debt, deducts interest, depreciates the machines, and pockets the spread. When the term ends, the same machines may be re-leased to smaller clinics or sold offshore, extending the yield curve.

Vehicle arbitrage works similarly but with lifestyle perks. A luxury car dealership principal sets up a separate entity that buys exotic cars and then leases them back to the dealership for test-drive fleets. Lease payments are deductible to the operating business; the leasing entity—owned by the principal—records revenue at a favorable tax rate and allows the owner personal use under a legitimate "demonstrator" policy.

Private lending is the quiet juggernaut. Wealthy individuals create note funds or single-member LLCs that issue hard-money loans at 10–15 % interest, secured by first-position liens on real-estate rehabs or inventory. Points and origination fees juice the effective yield. Defaults are rare because collateral value tops loan value; if a borrower walks away, the lender inherits an asset at a discount.

Inside retirement wrappers—self-directed IRAs or solo 401(k)s—those interest payments grow either tax-deferred or tax-free. Some families form **Reg D debt funds**, pooling investor capital to scale volume, then layering in senior–subordinate tranches so the family keeps the safest slice while outside investors chase yield.

The wealthy frequently **stack** strategies: they lend capital from Entity A to Entity B (which they also own) to purchase Equipment C, which is then leased to Operating Company D (another related entity). Interest flows one way, lease payments flow another, and depreciation lives in a third pocket. Each stream has unique tax treatment, and the web is designed so no single entity shows excessive profit—minimizing taxes, maximizing flexibility, and baffling competitors who try to reverse-engineer the economics.

Result: a latticework of revenue trickles—royalties, lease checks, interest coupons—quietly filling accounts every month. No boss. No timesheet. No social-media brag. Just the steady hum of capital doing what capital does best: reproducing in the dark, far from the noise of earned-income taxation.

How the Wealthy Turn Hobbies Into Write-Offs

Most people treat hobbies as discretionary spending—nice if you can afford them, first to be cut if money gets tight. The affluent see hobbies as an opportunity to re-categorize outlays from lifestyle costs to deductible business expenses. They don't "cheat" the tax code; they rewrite their leisure activities as bona fide enterprises that satisfy the IRS's profit-motive tests. The result is a life where virtually every passion project either pays for itself or, at minimum, lowers taxable income.

Consider private aviation. A mid-market entrepreneur might buy a jet for convenience, swallow the depreciation, and pay after-tax dollars for fuel and crew. A sophisticated owner sets up three entities:

1. **An aircraft-leasing LLC** that owns the plane and rents it to charter operators.

2. **An aviation consulting S-corp** that sells flight-department management services.

3. **A holding company** that invoices both entities for branding and logistics.

Each flight is coded as either charter revenue, deductible repositioning, or owner-business travel backed by board minutes. Hangar fees, pilot salaries, and maintenance reserves—all are ordinary and necessary expenses, drastically reducing the leasing LLC's taxable profit. Overnight, a "toy" becomes cash-flow neutral and shelters other active income via bonus depreciation (100 % write-off in year one for new or used aircraft placed in service).

Shift to art. A collector who spends $10 million on canvases can form a **private museum foundation** that loans pieces to public exhibitions. The foundation pays storage, insurance, and acquisition costs; the collector receives a charitable deduction for donating partial interests. When a piece appreciates, the foundation can license high-resolution images for textbooks or print runs—generating royalty income exempt from federal tax. The family gains cultural prestige, estate-tax reduction, and a steady revenue stream, all while the masterpieces hang in climate-controlled warehouses they effectively control.

Equestrian passions follow similar logic. Running a **breeding and training LLC** qualifies for agricultural deductions—feed, veterinary care, transportation, and even a portion of property taxes on the ranch. Prize money counts as revenue; stud fees create recurring cash flow. Losses in the start-up years can offset unrelated passive gains, provided the owner maintains books, a separate bank account, and a plausible business plan filed with the IRS.

Yachting? Register the vessel under a **foreign flag corporation**, charter it out 14 weeks a year, and recoup operating costs while logging personal voyages as repositioning for maintenance. Motorsports? Capitalize a **track-side data-analytics firm** that sells performance telemetry to other teams; the race car becomes R&D equipment, deductible under Section 179. Film production? Establish a **special-purpose vehicle (SPV)** to finance a documentary, claim state production tax credits, and sell distribution rights—turning vacation travel into location scouting.

The linchpin is **documentation plus intent**. The IRS's hobby-loss rules (Section 183) presume an activity is a hobby if it fails to show a profit in three of five years, but savvy advisors layer objective profit motives—market studies, professional management, recurring revenue projections—to defend deductions. Annual board meetings with minutes, separate accounting software, and third-party marketing efforts all reinforce legitimacy.

Ultimately, the wealthy ask: "How can this passion intersect with a market need?" A vineyard hosts corporate retreats, a car-collection clubhouse sells memberships, and a high-altitude trekking obsession morphs into a luxury adventure-travel brand. Leisure becomes a legacy when structured to create value for others—and value creation is always deductible.

Secret Uses of Life Insurance for Wealth Transfer and Borrowing

To the casual observer, life insurance is a grim safety net: pay premiums, die, let beneficiaries collect. Affluent families, however, use permanent life policies as multi-tool instruments for tax deferral, estate planning, and low-cost leverage. Properly engineered, a policy operates like a **private family bank** with statutory creditor protection and IRS-blessed tax treatment.

Start with **whole life** or **indexed universal life (IUL)**. Premium dollars are split into two buckets: the pure insurance cost and a cash-value account that grows tax-deferred. Carriers credit that account at fixed or equity-linked rates, but the policyholder's real benefit is access: most contracts allow **policy loans** up to 90 % of cash value at 2–4 % interest, no questions asked and no credit report pulled. Because a loan isn't income, there's no tax event. Meanwhile, the credited interest often continues to accrue on the full cash value, not the net amount after borrowing—creating positive arbitrage.

Example: a policy with a $2 million cash value earns a net 5 % internal rate. The owner borrows $1 million at 3 %, invests in real-estate syndication yielding 12 %, and pockets the 9-point spread while the policy keeps compounding. If the loan is never repaid, the outstanding balance simply reduces the death benefit—still delivered income-tax-free to heirs.

Enter **premium-financed life insurance**. Instead of tying up liquidity, a borrower secures bank financing for the majority of the premium outlay (often 60–80 %). The policy's cash value plus outside collateral covers the loan; the client pays only interest, typically less than 4 %. After 10 years, the rising cash value can fully collateralize and then retire the banknote, leaving the policy in force with minimal out-of-pocket cost. For estates facing 40 % federal tax, using leverage to create tax-free liquidity is a no-brainer.

Wealth managers also deploy insurance inside **irrevocable life insurance trusts (ILITs)**. Funding premiums via annual gift-tax exclusions shift assets out of the taxable estate. Upon death, the trust receives the death proceeds, buys illiquid family business shares from the estate at fair market value, and injects cash so heirs aren't forced to sell legacy assets to pay estate tax.

Beyond legacy, policies lubricate **buy-sell agreements** among business partners. Each owner's life is insured; if one dies, proceeds buy out the deceased's shares, preventing disruptive outside ownership. Executives negotiate **deferred compensation** plans wrapped in corporate-owned life policies (COLI). Employers get tax-favored growth; employees receive tax-free retirement supplements.

Even charitable planning benefits: a donor funds a life policy naming a foundation as beneficiary. The premium gifts are deductible; the eventual death benefit far exceeds the cumulative deductions, leveraging philanthropic impact.

Creditors and litigants also find insurance frustratingly unreachable. Many states shield cash values from judgments, making policies effective in **asset-protection vaults**. Combine with offshore trusts in jurisdictions like the Cook Islands, and the fortress becomes nearly impenetrable.

Stack insurance with other structures and possibilities multiply. A dynasty trust buys policies on multiple generations; loans from the trust finance beneficiary ventures; profits flow back, premiums get paid, and the cycle repeats. The IRS can see the pieces but rarely pierces the carefully layered intent.

In elite circles, life insurance is less about mortality and more about **capital choreography**: shifting liquidity, arbitraging rates, immunizing estates, and silently compounding value outside the taxable world. Pair that with the royalty streams, leases, and credit lines already described, and you have a portfolio where visible salary is optional—yet wealth grows faster than any paycheck could keep up.

Chapter 7 – Privacy as Power: How the Wealthy Erase Their Tracks

How to Vanish Financially Without Breaking the Law

Most people think transparency is the default condition of modern finance: if someone owns a mansion, a yacht, or a sizable brokerage account, surely it shows up on a title search or a "rich list." Yet true wealth engineers know that visibility is a design flaw, not a requirement. Privacy can be baked in from day one—legally—by separating every major asset from its beneficiary in ways that frustrate casual snooping and deter even well-funded litigants.

Begin with the **three-layer doctrine**:

- **Asset Layer** – the LLC, land trust, or Special Purpose Vehicle that directly holds real estate, aircraft, boats, bank or brokerage accounts, intellectual property, or crypto cold wallets.

- **Holding Layer** – a second-tier entity, often in a U.S. privacy state (Wyoming, Delaware, New Mexico) or a foreign jurisdiction with sealed corporate registries (Belize, Seychelles). This entity owns 100 % of the asset layer, so your name stays off county deeds, FAA registries, or FINRA records.

- **Beneficial Layer** – an irrevocable trust or foundation that owns the holding company. In South Dakota or Nevada, the trust deed is confidential; in the Cook Islands or Nevis, court orders from abroad are routinely ignored. You can serve as a protector—with a veto over trustee actions—without revealing yourself on any public filing.

By itself, entity layering removes your name from obvious searches. But metadata—mailing addresses, phone records, utility bills—can still connect the dots. Privacy pros therefore create **lifestyle cut-outs**:

- **Virtual mailboxes** scan and email correspondence; actual packages are forwarded through third-party couriers. No Amazon driver ever shows up at your real residence.

- **Corporate phone plans** link SIM cards to shell entities. Caller ID traces back to the LLC, not to you.

- **Prepaid debit cards** feed from entity bank accounts for day-to-day purchases; statements list the business address.

Financial footprints shrink further through **payment dispersion**. Utility bills go on the property LLC's card, not yours. Car insurance drafts from a vehicular-leasing LLC. Streaming subscriptions debit a media-consulting S-corp. If an investigator subpoenas your personal bank statements, they find little more than grocery runs.

Next is **jurisdictional hardening**. Place liquid reserves in a Swiss, Liechtenstein, or Singaporean private bank under the name of your Cook Islands trust. Add a Nevis LLC as a managing member to inject another layer. Now any litigant must fight a multi-front war: sue you in domestic court, pierce the Wyoming company, challenge the South Dakota trust, and then retain foreign counsel to chase assets offshore—an exercise that can cost six or seven figures upfront with no guarantee of payoff.

Finally, observe **discipline**. Never sign personally if an authorized officer can. Never provide a Social Security number when an EIN suffices. Use encrypted messaging (Signal, Proton Mail) for sensitive coordination with attorneys and registered agents. Keep separate laptops for entity management—air-gapped from social media to avoid accidental metadata leaks.

The end state isn't criminal secrecy; it's **lawful obscurity**. You still pay taxes, file K-1s, and disclose foreign accounts on FBARs—only the IRS and your CPA know the full picture. Everyone else sees a mirage of modest means, discouraging lawsuits, kidnappings, tabloid interest, or political grandstanding. Privacy, in this sense, is preventive security—and the highest form of luxury is to live unbothered.

The Power of Nominee Structures and Privacy Jurisdictions

Nominees add a human shield to the entity labyrinth, supplying names and signatures so yours never appear in searchable databases. But nominees are only as good as the jurisdictions that empower them, so sophisticated planners combine the two for near-impenetrable anonymity.

How nominees work in practice

1. **Nominee Director** – A licensed professional is appointed to the board of your BVI or Seychelles company. Public filings list their name; internal resolutions delegate all management authority back to you via a private power-of-attorney. They attend annual meetings—often by video—and sign minutes prepared by your counsel.

2. **Nominee Shareholder** – Shares are issued in the nominee's name and held under a declaration of trust. Dividends route to a bank account you control (through the holding layer), leaving no public breadcrumb.

3. **Nominee Settlor** – For trusts, a third party can execute the initial settlement and immediately resign. The true grantor is inserted later via a deed of appointment, unrecorded anywhere but the trustee's vault.

Jurisdictions that super-charge nominees

- **Belize** – Permits international business companies (IBCs) with bearer shares and no public registry of owners or directors. Annual fees stay low; accounting books can be kept anywhere in the world.

- **Nevis** – LLC statutes protect managers from court-ordered turnovers; charging orders are the exclusive remedy for creditors, making collection nearly impossible.

- **Seychelles** – Allows hybrid foundations: part trust, part corporation, ideal for holding IP or yachts. Founder details stay sealed; only the charter is public.

- **South Dakota & Wyoming** – Inside the U.S., these states rival offshore havens. South Dakota offers directed trusts with perpetual duration and automatic seal of court records. Wyoming provides lifetime charging-order protection for single-member LLCs.

Layering tactics

A favorite structure for intellectual-property heavy businesses is:
IP Holding Ltd. (Seychelles Foundation) → owns **Wyoming LLC** → licenses trademarks to **Delaware C-Corp** that operates the e-commerce brand. Royalties flow from Delaware (21 % federal tax rate) to Wyoming (no state tax), then cross-charge to Seychelles where a territorial regime taxes foreign income at 0 %. Public databases show only the Delaware company; deeper digging hits the Wyoming firewall; beyond that, foreign privacy laws stall the trail.

Mitigating the risk of nominee failure

Sophisticated families implement **redundant control instruments**: dual powers-of-attorney, springing members who appear if a nominee dies, and encrypted escrow of critical documents with separate law firms on different continents. They schedule annual "fire drills" to rehearse replacing a director within 48 hours, ensuring banking authority remains uninterrupted.

Cost-benefit calculus

Nominee packages range from $500 per year for a Wyoming LLC manager to $5,000+ in offshore jurisdictions with FATCA compliance support. For a net worth north of $10 million, the price is trivial relative to potential lawsuit judgments, extortion attempts, or political targeting.

Legality and optics

Regulators recognize legitimate uses—corporate raiders hiding accumulation of target-company shares, celebrities shielding home addresses, dissidents protecting family assets. Abuse arises only if nominees conceal criminal proceeds. Maintaining audited books, filing accurate tax returns, and observing substance requirements keep structures squarely within the law.

The net effect is **structural invisibility** without sacrificing control. You still steer the ship; you simply sail under a flag that radar can't lock onto. And in a world where data breaches, cancel culture, and weaponized litigation grow daily, staying off the radar is no longer arrogance—it's self-defense.

Financial Obfuscation: Making Yourself a Small Target

"Own nothing, control everything" is more than an aphorism—it's an engineering manual. A creditor, journalist, or angry ex-partner can only strike what they can see; if your balance sheet looks thin and scattered, you're not worth the legal fees. The wealthy therefore pursue **three converging tactics— fragmentation, conversion, and camouflage—until their economic footprint collapses into a statistical rounding error.**

1 | Fragmentation: atomize every pocket of value

- **Vertical chains** – A land trust owns a single-property LLC; that LLC is owned by a Delaware series unit; the series is held by a Wyoming holding company; voting units rest in a South Dakota-directed trust. One subpoena reveals only the land trust; five jurisdictions protect the rest.

- **Horizontal dispersion** – Instead of one brokerage with $20 million, there are eight accounts below $2.5 million each: two in Zurich, one in Singapore, two in Liechtenstein foundations, one inside a Bermuda segregated account company, plus a gold-backed note in Dubai. Each lies under a different reporting threshold or treaty.

- **Time-slice entities** – A new LLC forms for every major contract, then dissolves when the deal ends. Even if someone proves the shell once held cash, there's nothing left to seize.

2 | Conversion: swap obvious income for opaque streams

Payroll is kryptonite—it creates W-2 trials, garnish-able wages, and lifestyle assumptions. The affluent convert it into:

- **Management fees** from a consulting C-corp that invoices their operating companies. Shifting profit to the corporation means personal 1040s show minimal adjusted gross income.

- **Policy loans**—cash borrowed from whole-life insurance at 3 % and spent freely, never reported as income, never subject to Schedule B or C scrutiny.

- **Private-placement life-settlement funds** distribute long-term capital gains (at favorable rates) rather than ordinary income.

- **Tax-exempt muni-bond ladders** inside grantor trusts; coupons skip the 1099 INT trail because they flow to the trust, not the individual.

3 | Camouflage: wrap lifestyle assets in business logic

A townhouse is re-zoned as a corporate hospitality space and booked as a marketing expense. A 100-foot yacht is chartered through a Marshall-Island company 14 weeks a year; the IRS safe-harbor for "ordinary and necessary" charter operations converts fuel, crew, and dockage into deductible costs. Vintage cars reside in a Delaware statutory trust filed as "inventory of a museum start-up" and appear on the owner's Instagram only when cross-tagged as promotional media for that museum.

4 | Banking and payment opacity

Private banks in Switzerland and Luxembourg issue multi-currency debit cards linked to the entity, not the signer. Wire instructions hide the underlying owner through "omnibus client accounts." Daily expenses route through prepaid cards topped up by an offshore PCC (protected cell company) whose individual cells are legally remote from one another—so even if one cell faces a claim, the float in other cells is safe.

5 | Legal pressure testing

An in-house counsel simulates litigation: can a hypothetical claimant trace from lawsuit to asset in fewer than six motions? If the answer is yes, yet another entity layer is inserted, or a domestic asset-protection trust migrates to the Cook Islands, where fraudulent transfer statutes of limitation expire in 24 months.

By the end, a plaintiff's attorney discovers only nominal checking accounts, leased residences, and personal effects of modest declared value. The real economics pulse safely behind a hall of mirrors—perfectly reported to tax authorities, yet functionally unreachable to everyone else. **Obfuscation isn't illegal; it's a cost-benefit strategy that makes aggression irrational.**

The Reason You Can't Find Their Name on Anything

Google, Zillow, county clerks, DMV databases—each promises a breadcrumb trail from a person to their possessions. But for elite planners, every breadcrumb is swept away long before outsiders start looking. **Direct ownership is a neon "sue me" sign; proxy control is an invisibility cloak.**

Architecting the Ghost Profile

1. **Title scrubbing** – Personal names vanish from deeds via land trusts; trustees of record are law firm clerks bound by confidentiality. Vehicle titles list a Montana LLC (exploiting zero sales tax) managed by a Nevada series company. The FAA aircraft registry shows a Delaware trust company as owner trustee—a standard practice that masks beneficiary identity.

2. **Equity dilution** – A tech founder places super-voting shares into an irrevocable grantor trust before Series B. Subsequent pro-rata investments occur through an offshore SPV. Public S-1 filings later list shares under "Entities affiliated with XYZ Trust"; the founder shows minimal personal stake, shielding both net-worth estimates and potential

activist-investor attacks.

3. **Digital minimalism** – Personal domain registrations use privacy proxies; social accounts link to a media LLC. Residence Wi-Fi is in a staff member's name; smart-home devices route through a corporate VPN. Data brokers sell nothing beyond a P.O. box and a 10-year-old Honda.

4. **Transactional fog** – High-value art is bought via art-factoring lines; invoices show a Gibraltarian free-port address. Credit card points fund first-class travel booked through a concierge service that bills to a marketing company. Hotel check-ins use alias corporate names for "brand-evaluation research."

5. **Philanthropy as a vault** – A $100 million private foundation owns 20 % of a for-profit LLC that manages renewable-energy assets. The foundation's 990 lists only aggregate numbers; the founder's name appears once on page 7 under "interested persons," not as an owner. Media praises the generosity, never realizing the structure multiplies the fortune tax-free.

Legal Underpinnings

- **Charging-order exclusivity** in states like Wyoming prevents creditors from seizing LLC assets; they can only wait for distributions that may never come.

- **Statutory secrecy** in South Dakota seals trust proceedings; even heirs can be kept in the dark until vesting ages.

- **Bearer-share or unsettled foundations** in jurisdictions such as Panama or Liechtenstein allow economic rights to pass hand-to-hand without registry amendments, bypassing reporting thresholds.

Outcome: structural untraceability

You cannot subpoena what is outside domestic jurisdiction. You cannot garnish wages that don't exist. You cannot lien an estate that shows a negligible probate inventory because everything substantive was retitled years earlier. **Risk is deflected to empty shells; wealth operates off-stage.**

Courts uphold it because statutes, revenue rulings, and decades of case law enshrine each step. Legislators leave loopholes intact because their blind trustees use identical playbooks. In effect, the wealthy haven't gamed the system—they've **sponsored** it.

In an era when one tweet can ignite a boycott, one hacker can leak a database, and one lawsuit can freeze personal accounts, invisibility is no longer vanity; it's a survival strategy. For those who can afford the architects, **anonymity is engineered, audited, and stress-tested—then quietly enjoyed for generations.**

Chapter 8 – The Psychological Codes of the Elite

Thinking in Net Worth, Not Income

Ask a roomful of high earners to state their financial goal and most will quote a salary figure: $150 K, $500 K, maybe $1 M. Now ask a roomful of millionaires and billionaires, and they answer with a balance-sheet number: $10 M net worth, $100 M in equity, $1 B in enterprise value. The contrast reveals the primary psychological rift between ordinary achievers and the truly wealthy: **one group counts paychecks and the other counts ownership.**

When you fixate on income, you naturally design your life around labor inputs: longer hours, advanced degrees, overtime, and side hustles. Every upgrade in lifestyle demands more hours or a higher rate. Your time becomes the choke point of prosperity. Worse, the tax code punishes earned income most severely—ordinary rates, payroll taxes, and phase-outs. A six-figure earner can still live month-to-month.

Net-worth thinkers reverse the sequence. They look first at their **balance sheet**—assets minus liabilities—then ask, "What deal, acquisition, or restructure lifts that number fastest?" A $200 K condo down payment might add only $50 K to net worth (equity). That same $200 K backing a 20 % stake in a cash-flowing small business could add $1 M to net worth on day one, plus distributions. Same cash outlay but, a radically different balance-sheet impact. That is how elite minds triage opportunities.

They maintain **dashboards, not budgets**. A family office controller produces monthly statements: total equity by asset class, loan-to-value ratios, unrealized gains, liquidity coverage, and credit capacity. Income appears only as a footnote—useful but secondary. If net worth dips because of market drawdowns, the question isn't "How do we cut expenses?" but "Which distressed asset can we buy at a 40 % discount to restore the curve?"

This lens alters **career strategy**. Top lawyers and doctors trade billable hours for cash; equity thinkers trade sweat for stock. An engineer can accept $80 K plus 1 % of a high-growth start-up. If that company exits at $500 M, the engineer's equity is $5 M—an after-tax haul impossible to replicate via salary alone.

Risk tolerance shifts too. Income-centric earners dread temporary pay cuts; net-worth builders will forgo salary for years to accumulate outsized stakes. That's why founders often pay themselves $1 during scale phases yet become cent millionaires at exit.

Tax behavior follows suit. Paycheck people chase deductible donations and 401(k) limits. Owners pursue **step-ups in basis, 1031 swaps, QSBS exclusions, and carried-interest treatment**—tools that vaporize six or seven figures of tax on capital events. A $3 M salary earner might surrender $1 M to tax; a $3 M capital gainer can often owe less than $300 K—or roll the gain entirely.

Even **liquidity planning** changes. Instead of keeping six months' salary in cash, the wealthy favor **credit backstops** against portfolio assets. A $2 M securities-based line of credit at 4 % costs $80 K annually if fully drawn—far cheaper than parking $2 M in idle cash. They ensure liquidity, not with savings, but with leverage capacity. That keeps maximum dollars compounding inside the balance sheet.

Most importantly, net-worth focus frees time. Once assets throw off enough passive cash to cover lifestyle costs, the owner's calendar opens for vision work: raising a new fund, mentoring successors, or simply living. Paradoxically, obsessing about balance sheets instead of income statements produces more discretionary time.

Shift your daily metrics. Track **total equity, net cash flow, asset yield, and weighted tax rate**. Evaluate new endeavors by balance-sheet impact first, cashflow second, and labor requirement last. Do that consistently, and within five years you'll think, speak, and invest like the top 1 %.

Delayed Gratification Is a Myth (Used Against You)

"Live frugally for forty years and retire at sixty-five" is preached as a financial gospel, but it's designed for people whose only wealth engine is wages. The elite reject that timetable outright. They want first-class flights this quarter—funded by assets that keep compounding. They don't postpone pleasure; they **monetize pleasure** so it finances itself.

Start with the myth's fallacy: it assumes resources are **finite** and consumption erodes the pile. For owners of scalable assets, resources are replenishing. A beach villa rented to luxury travelers can pay its mortgage, fund the owner's vacations, and still appreciate 5–7 % annually. The villa isn't an indulgence; it's an ATM.

Wealthy families adopt a **yield-buys-lifestyle formula**:

1. **Price the desire** – $60 K per year for global travel.
2. **Select an asset class** – multifamily LP stakes yielding 8 % net.
3. **Back-solve principal** – $60 K ÷ 0.08 = $750 K investment.
4. **Acquire with leverage** – Put $250 K down, finance the rest, and use depreciation to offset distributions.

Now the travel budget is perpetual and tax-favored. No guilt, no depletion—just asset-funded living.

This principle scales to automobiles, tuition, and philanthropic pledges. Instead of paying cash for a $200 K EV, an investor drops $200 K into a short-term real-estate debt fund at 12 %. The $24 K annual interest leases the car; the principal stays intact. When the lease ends, the fund principal is redeployed to finance the next luxury—or another asset.

Even time gratification accelerates. The average worker saves vacation days; a net-worth mindset outsources operations early, buying calendar freedom in their thirties. They hire estate managers, EAs, and fractional CFOs. Their cost of delegation is paid by portfolio yield, not forfeited salary. Thus "retirement" happens piecemeal: Fridays first, then months, until work becomes optional.

Critics call this reckless leverage. In reality, it's **asset-liability matching**: aligning a stable yield source with a recurring expense. Risk is mitigated by diversification and insurance. If one cash-flow engine falters, another picks up the slack, or lifestyle scales temporarily—never principal.

Delayed-gratification dogma also ignores **mortality math**. A luxury safari at age thirty-five is a memory asset; the same trip at seventy may be physically impossible. The wealthy front-load peak-experience years, ensuring health intersects with means. They'd rather refinance a property to seize a once-in-a-lifetime yacht passage than hoard equity for heirs who can build their own.

Finally, the myth shows **obedience**. If you're always waiting, you're easy to manage—accept paltry raises, buy target-date funds, and defer dreams. Owners break that spell by proving assets can pay for desires today. Each proof-of-concept (dividends cover Porsche lease, option premiums pay kids' private school) erodes scarcity conditioning and fuels bigger visions.

The takeaway is not a license for reckless spending. It's a call to redirect all desire toward **cash-flow acquisition**. Want a $10 K watch? Secure a dividend stream that nets $10 K annually, then buy the watch guilt-free. Want a sabbatical? Create passive income to replace the salary you'll forgo. Convert every wish list into an asset target, and delayed gratification morphs into **engineered gratification**—luxury now, compounded wealth later.

Playing Long-Term Games with Unfair Advantages

"A year goes fast; a decade decides destinies." The affluent internalize that mantra early because compounding rewards only reveal their full force over long horizons. Yet patience alone isn't their superpower. They salt their timelines with **structural edges** that hard-wire outperformance: cheaper capital, insider access, bespoke tax codes, and armies of specialists who keep the flywheel spinning while they sleep.

Begin with **capital stack asymmetry**. A small developer might finance a project with 10 % hard-money loans at 70 % loan-to-value. A billionaire's family office taps an A-rated bond issue at 2 % or friendly bank credit secured by a $200 M equity portfolio. When both hold the asset for ten years, appreciation is similar, but the carrying cost gap widens the rich investor's IRR by hundreds of basis points—an invisible boost that compounds quarter after quarter.

Add **information on lead time**. Zoning-board agenda packets are public, but few amateurs read them. A land-banking syndicate retains ex-city planners to flag corridor expansions years in advance. They quietly option adjoining parcels, lobby for infrastructure, and wait. When the retail press finally predicts a "hot corridor," the syndicate is already filing for entitlements. Ten-for-one gains look magical but arise from legally obtained, early-cycle data.

The control premium is another lever. The wealthy don't merely buy shares; they buy the board seat. A mid-market private equity shop acquires 60 % of a precision parts manufacturer, inserts a Six Sigma veteran as CEO, and signs a supply deal with an aerospace portfolio company it already owns. EBITDA tripled in three years—not because the industry boomed, but because governance, procurement, and cross-selling were orchestrated top-down. Public shareholders can't replicate that.

Moreover, the elite investors' structure exists to recycle capital tax-free. A property can be 1031-exchanged into a larger asset; a portfolio company sold into an **opportunity-zone fund** defers or eliminates gains; a tech founder rolls sale proceeds into **Qualified Small Business Stock** of the next disruptor and wipes out $10 M of future gains entirely. Patience multiplies, but tax technology supercharges the multiplier.

They even **buy time wholesale**. A surgeon works eighty-hour weeks; a venture capitalist hires two associates for diligence, a fractional CFO for modeling, a law firm on retainer for term sheets, and spends her hours on conference floors extracting proprietary deal flow. Every salaried stranger she hires turns into extra future years of her life—redeployed to high-sigma choices instead of rote tasks. That is the true cost of capital: using dollars to hoard years.

Risk management also shifts with the horizon. Short-term traders panic over a 15 % drawdown; a timberland fund expects wildfires and bugs, yet models wood growth over forty-year harvest cycles. Insurance wrappers, interest-rate swaps, and even political-risk guarantees (via the World Bank's MIGA program) insulate long plays from exogenous shocks. To onlookers, outcomes seem pre-ordained; in reality, the downside was off-loaded to counterparties at pennies on the dollar.

Critically, long-game players embed **auto-ratchets**: set-and-forget triggers that step up an advantage as the scale grows. Debt covenants may automatically reduce interest rates once EBITDA crosses thresholds. Mezzanine tranches convert to common at preferential caps. Supplier agreements lock volume pricing a decade out. By the time competitors notice, the elite player enjoys—not just a head start—but accelerating distance.

Contrast that with paycheck chasers. They switch jobs for a 7 % raise, shift 401(k) allocations quarterly, and refinance the house every time rates drop. Each move is defensive, episodic, and largely taxable. Their 30-year outlook is an act of faith. The long-game elite, in contrast, program destiny: compounders baked in, incentives aligned, time converted from foe to ally.

Long-term thinking is often romanticized as patient stoicism. In truth, its clinical opportunism stretched across decades—bolstered by cheat codes that most players never unlock. Anyone can extend the horizon; few can pair it with discount capital, inside pricing, and stacked downside shields. That's why the richest families rarely need to gamble; they just engineer inevitability.

Why the Wealthy Stay Quiet About Wealth

Money talks—but the loudest voice usually belongs to someone still trying to prove they have it. Old fortunes operate on a different frequency: hushed, indirect, and, to outsiders, curiously absent from obvious registries. This silence isn't modesty. It's a **risk-adjusted communication strategy** refined over generations.

First, visibility is an invitation to **predatory litigation**. Tort lawyers scrape public deeds and cap tables to size targets. An LLC-owned loft and minimal W-2 income discourage contingency cases. A braggy headline about a $50 M windfall does the opposite. Even frivolous suits cost six figures to dismiss; stealth is cheaper than victory.

Second, publicity distorts **deal flow**. Announce a big exit and suddenly bankers pitch overpriced SPACs, friends request angel checks, and every social acquaintance peddles a "can't miss" prototype. Quiet capital is choosy; loud capital gets carpet-bombed by opportunities so bad insiders already passed. By staying mute, the wealthy curate inbound pitches organically—through law firms, club deals, and vetted peers—filtering noise before it reaches their inboxes.

Third, silence maintains **pricing power**. Suppose a landowner plans a multi-parcel assemblage. If rumor spreads she's a billionaire, holdouts raise the price. If she approaches via an acquisition vehicle with an average-income mailing address, parcels transact at fair market. Similar dynamics apply in art auctions, aircraft charters, and even political donations (dark-money 501(c)(4)s avoid bidding wars for influence).

Fourth, psychological distance protects relationships. Mention a portfolio's nine-figure value at dinner, and every comment thereafter is colored by envy, flattery, or resentment. Under-state, and friends engage authentically. Elite parents teach children to dress neutrally, drive unobtrusive cars, and never quote trust-fund balances. Money that isn't paraded retains **social agility**.

Fifth, regulatory heat follows headlines. A quiet billionaire can lobby discreetly; a Twitter-obsessed one draws activist campaigns and congressional subpoenas. Consider the contrasting trajectories of low-profile retail heirs versus outspoken tech founders. Both wield influence, but the latter endures antitrust probes, personal-data exposés, and open-mic gaffes forwarded to regulators. **Stealth is compliance insurance**.

Finally, opportunity gravitates to silence because insiders communicate via a signal, not a billboard. Lawyers know which family offices close quickly. Fund managers track whose LP commitments show up before the first close. These circles value reliability over publicity, and discretion is the unspoken handshake that grants a perpetual first look.

To replicate:

- **Speak through entities**—press releases cite the LLC or foundation, never the individual.

- **Outsource spotlight**—let project CEOs, portfolio founders, or museum curators take interviews. Your equity stays footnoted.

- **Default to NDAs**—family-office visitors sign before touring. Conference talks go off-record.

- **Train heirs**—vacations are Instagram-free zones; philanthropy is branded under cause, not a surname.

- **Use reputation pivots**—public persona is "local investor" or "art patron," never "crypto whale" or "options wizard."

Quiet wealth compounds because it sidesteps friction—legal, social, and political. Noise consumes bandwidth and invites predators; silence preserves optionality. In an oversharing age, reticence is radical power: the less your name circulates, the fewer obstacles appear between you and the next asymmetric move.

As you build, remember: **the best brag is a balance sheet no one sees but everyone feels**.

Chapter 9 – Breaking In: How You Start Using These Tactics Without a Fortune

Where to Begin With Limited Capital

"I'll start acting like the wealthy once I have real money" is backward thinking. They got real money because they acted wealthy—structurally, mentally, and strategically—while funds were still tight. You can begin that same shift with three guiding questions: **What can I own? How can I shield it? Who can I leverage?**

Own something—anything—that's not your labor.
Digital footholds cost almost nothing. Buy a domain and publish evergreen tutorials; license the content under a paywall. Self-publish a 40-page e-book and attach a perpetual affiliate link. Create a small Shopify store targeting a micro-niche and outsource fulfillment. Even $100 a month in automated profit is your first non-salary asset.

Physical micro-assets exist too. Pool $5,000 with friends to buy a used vending machine and place it in a busy salon. Acquire a cash-flowing Kindle title or a tiny YouTube channel on a marketplace. These are not get-rich schemes; they are skill gyms that teach ownership mechanics—contracts, revenue splits, and tax treatment—on training-wheels scale.

Shield the new asset immediately.
You can file an LLC in Wyoming for under $300 including a registered agent. Use it as the payment merchant, the ad-revenue recipient, or the vending machine landlord. Obtain an EIN and open a free business checking account. You're now eligible for business credit cards—0 % APR periods, category bonuses, and sign-up rewards stack leverage before your cash balance grows.

Leverage other people's balance sheets.
Local community banks thirst for small commercial loans. Open a $1,000 secured line, pay it off monthly, and graduate to an unsecured $25 K credit line

within a year. Vendors often extend NET-30 terms once they see an LLC, EIN, and a basic website. These relationships cost nothing but attention and position you for larger plays—inventory financing, equipment leasing, or bridge loans—when scale arrives.

Exploit tax code freebies.
A side LLC lets you deduct a home-office portion of the rent, cell phone, internet, and software. Contribute $6,500 to a Roth IRA or, better, open a Solo 401(k) once the LLC shows a profit. Contribute 20 % of net income pre-tax—money that would otherwise bleed away.

Stack knowledge aggressively.
Subscribe to niche deal-flow newsletters, join local chamber mastermind lunches, and volunteer at angel-network pitch events. Pay attention to term-sheet vocabulary—liquidation preference, warrants, SAFE caps—long before you write big checks. Information asymmetry favors whoever studies earliest.

Automate capital capture.
Set up an auto-transfer: 10 % of every invoice hits a high-yield business savings account. Your first $10 K becomes the LP check for a micro-fund or the earnest money deposit on a duplex. Capital tends to gather where systems escort it—never leave this to "leftover" income.

Mindset checkpoint: If your wage job terminates tomorrow but the vending machine, the e-book, and the YouTube royalties keep paying, you've already exited the all-labor trap. Scale each stream by 10 × and you're free. The wealthy just run this play at $1 M, $10 M, $100 M magnitude—but the DNA is identical.

The Power of Structure Before Scale

The structure is the scaffolding that lets tiny ventures morph into durable empires. Picture two food-truck owners each netting $75 K. One operates under his Social Security number and a shoebox ledger; the other formed "StreetBite Holdings LLC," tracks expenses in QuickBooks, has a DUNS number, liability insurance, and a cash-balance SEP IRA. When a regional mall offers a food court lease, only one is bankable—the structured one—because bankers, landlords, and investors read the organization as a proxy for competence.

Blueprint for sub-$1 k setup

- **Choose jurisdiction smartly.** Live in California? File a manager-managed Wyoming LLC to avoid the $800 franchise tax; qualify as a foreign entity if/when revenue justifies it. Total registration cost: about $300.

- **Draft operating agreements early.** Even single-member LLCs benefit: they outline succession if you're incapacitated, easing lender comfort.

- **Segregate accounts on day one.** Open free business checking and a rewards credit card. Run every expense through these to build credit data for future lending algorithms.

- **Bookkeep monthly.** A $13 subscription to Wave or a simple Airtable base categorizes inflows/outflows by project. Twelve clean statements impress underwriters more than top-line volume.

- **Payroll yourself.** Use a platform like Gusto to run even $300/month owner draws. Generates pay stubs—useful when qualifying for mortgages—while keeping distributions separate.

Identity separation multiplies leverage.
Adopt a neutral brand ("North-Bridge Ventures LLC") for client invoices; route phone calls to a Zoom number; use a virtual address service that scans mail. Privacy makes you look larger, mitigates personal-info scraping, and prevents would-be litigants from sizing your pockets.

Documentation = deal-readiness.
Keep a digital vault: articles of organization, EIN letters, annual minutes, tax

returns, insurance certificates, and NDAs. When an angel-group portal or SBA lender requests diligence, you respond in minutes, not weeks—perceived as "institutional" despite tiny revenue.

Tax engineering from dollar one

With structure, you can elect S-corp status once net profit exceeds about $40 K, potentially saving $5 K–$10 K in self-employment tax annually. You can hire your minor children for legitimate tasks—photo editing, packaging—and shift $13,850 per child tax-free (the 2025 standard deduction) into Roth IRAs.

Blueprint scales instantly

Add a short-term rental? Create a series cell or subsidiary LLC under the holding company. Launch an online course? Plug Stripe into your existing accounting category and apply for a higher-limit merchant advance based on historic LLC revenue. Want to syndicate a duplex? Draft a Regulation D subscription agreement—your cap-table template is already tested.

Signal effects

Attorneys return calls faster, banks waive fees, and suppliers approve NET-60 when your email signature shows "CFO" instead of "owner." Structure precedes perception; perception precedes opportunity.

Remember: growth stresses whatever foundation you pour it on. **Cheap structure early avoids expensive triage later**—no retroactive entity conversions, no messy commingled statements during due diligence. With the legal shell ready, every new venture becomes a plug-and-play module rather than a fire drill. Wealthy families learned this a century ago; you can learn it before your next paycheck hits.

Leveraging Information, Relationships, and Access

Cash is oxygen, but the information is altitude. If you can see a storm before others, you're airborne while competitors are still taxiing. Elite families devote a slice of every budget to intelligence—newsletters at $5,000 a year, legal updates, and sector-specific data feeds. You can emulate that edge on a shoestring by curating the right **signal stack**.

Start by deleting mass-market news apps that summarize yesterday's headlines. Replace them with:

• Free SEC RSS feeds filtered for Form D and 8-K filings—early hints of private raises and distressed sellers.
  • Podcast transcripts of earnings calls from micro-cap CEOs; they reveal supply-chain bottlenecks and vendor lists months before trade magazines.
  • CourtListener alerts on new tax-court dockets—front-row seats to real-world loophole litigation.
  • Niche subreddits and Discords where insiders dissect SBA lending hacks, local industrial auctions, or seller-financed cash-flow sites.

Layer paid intelligence as budget permits: a regional M&A newsletter ($29/month), a token-allocation tracker for early crypto rounds, or a property-auction API for under-market land. Within six weeks your browser home page will look like a miniature family-office terminal.

But data without context is noise. You need prolonged proximity to people deploying that data for profit. Consider a **value-for-access exchange**:

• Offer pro-bono competitive mapping or AI automation audits to local business-broker shops. They will repay you with first-look at pocket listings.
  • Volunteer as a notetaker for angel-group due-diligence teams; you'll read term sheets and lawyers' comments for free.
  • Code a dashboard for a solo GP raising a micro-fund; in return, secure an LP slot you couldn't normally afford.

Geography no longer limits access. Twitter Spaces, Clubhouse rooms, and private Zoom salons run by GP scouts are wide open between 10 p.m. and 2 a.m. Make incisive comments, clip transcripts, and publish takeaways within an hour—organizers will notice and DM you.

Craft a **digital footprint** that compounds. Post one in-depth thread a week breaking down a live private offering memorandum, a creative trust deed, or a capital-stack waterfall from a public S-1. Use plain English, cite statutes, and diagram flows. Within months, attorneys and deal sponsors will tag you for commentary, which drags you into deeper circles.

Remember, elite rooms operate on **credibility heuristics**: speed of response, quality of insights, and discretion. If you receive a PDF deck under NDA and summarize it on social media, you're out. But deliver a concise risk matrix to the sponsor in 24 hours and keep silent publicly—you're now "family."

Finally, forge **lattice connections** rather than vertical ones. A single mentor is helpful; a web of weak-tie allies is exponential. Your tax-litigation friend knows a title-escrow veteran who introduces you to a 1031 intermediary who knows four accredited co-investors. Each node multiplies optionality. Keep detailed notes—full names, children's schools, favorite obsessions—and follow up quarterly with relevant intel. This invisible CRM becomes your access machine, assembled at zero cost.

Information, relationships, and access operate as a flywheel: better intel earns you smarter commentary; smarter commentary earns you warmer intros; warmer intros position you closer to proprietary deals; those deals create case studies that make your commentary even more valuable. Money enters the loop later—almost as a side effect.

What You Need to Unlearn—and What to Master Next

Before you layer sophistication, you must excavate the mental concrete poured by mass culture. Begin a deliberate purge.

Unlearn the equation "High income equals security." Doctors earning $500 K can be wiped out by disability or malpractice. Landlords with ten four-plexes at 70 % LTV can remain wealthy while unconscious in a hospital. Security is passive equity, not active effort.

Unlearn "All debt is risky." Consumer debt destroys futures; asset-backed, tax-efficient leverage accelerates them. Study amortization tables: a $100 K HELOC rotated annually into a self-storage syndication can build $1 M net worth in a decade with less dollar risk than maxing out a 401(k).

Unlearn "Complex equals dangerous." Your cellphone is complex yet user-friendly because engineers abstracted the difficulty. View legal entities likewise. If your eyes glaze over at Internal Revenue Code § 754 elections, hire a CPA who loves that stuff. Complexity outsourced is strategy retained.

Unlearn "Rules are fixed." Congress rewrites depreciation schedules, estate-tax thresholds, and SEC accreditation definitions every cycle. Lobbyists craft carve-outs. Regulators issue private-letter rulings. The game board changes annually; winners refresh playbooks faster than textbooks update.

Now pivot to mastery.

Master **entity choreography**: the dance of operating LLCs, holding companies, and trusts. Sketch ownership diagrams until you can explain flow-through taxation, charging-order protection, and step-up in basis to a twelve-year-old.

Master **capital arbitrage**: securing credit at single-digit cost and deploying into double-digit ROI vehicles. Practice on a $15 K 0 % APR card buying liquidation pallets resold via Amazon FBA; graduate to SBA-7(a) loans for cash-flow businesses.

Master **deal-triage frameworks**: IRR vs. equity multiple, recourse vs. non-recourse, preferred returns, waterfalls, clawbacks. Teach these metrics once to a peer group; teaching locks knowledge.

Master **narrative positioning**. Curate LinkedIn to reflect strategic pursuits: "Acquisitions | PropTech | Micro PE." Publish quarterly letters—even if no LPs yet—to train your brain in institutional syntax. Perception precedes permission.

Master **governance**. Draft meeting minutes, board resolutions, and member consents, even for single-member entities. It's inexpensive discipline that inoculates you against veil-piercing claims later.

Master **lateral thinking in tax**: read biographies of billionaires' estate-tax battles; note the creative instruments—GRATs, CRUTs, IDGTs—they deployed. Then test one idea in miniature, like gifting $15 K of appreciated stock to a donor-advised fund.

Finally, master **emotional detachment**. Deals collapse, partners betray, markets crash. Wealth builders review lessons, patch protocols, and re-deploy. The version of you who shrugs off a $10 K loss will someday shrug off a $1 M paper hit—because your architecture can absorb shocks.

Awareness is phase one; structured action is phase two. Decide which unlearn-item dies this week and which mastery skill begins. Set a recurring calendar block titled "Owner's Hour" to refine entities, review credit lines, or map relationships. The masses hope compounding will save them; you will **engineer** it.

The blueprint is now public. Whether you execute quietly or default back to wage gravity is the choice that separates spectators from architects.

The Game Is Rigged - Play It Anyway

By now you've seen the curtain pulled back: different tax brackets are only the surface of a much wider chasm in rules, language, and opportunity. "Fairness" is marketed like a soft drink—easy to believe, profitable for the system—while the real operating manual stays behind closed doors. Taxes, liability shields, insider deal flow, jurisdictional loopholes, subsidized credit, regulatory carve-outs: every one of these leans toward those who already understand the architecture.

So frustration is natural. You may feel robbed of years spent coupon-clipping, celebrating 3 % raises, and dutifully funneling surplus into mutual funds that barely outran inflation. Yet outrage alone is unproductive; it burns energy but produces no equity. The pivotal insight is that **knowledge of the rigging is power in itself**: once you see the trap, you can step around it—or repurpose it as a springboard.

Remember, the elite weren't issued a different constitution. They simply receive different briefings—briefings you now possess. The statutes you once viewed as obstacles are the same statutes that let a restaurateur depreciate a remodel in one year, that allow a land investor to defer capital gains indefinitely, that justify a family office paying single-digit effective tax rates on fortunes hundreds of times larger than yours. **No gatekeeper physically bars you from these clauses; only unfamiliarity does.**

Your first strategic move is to convert awareness into a personal mandate. Instead of measuring unfairness, begin mapping leverage points. Schedule a "wealth sprint" weekend: line-by-line audit of your last three years' returns, entity gap analysis, credit-capacity check, estate-planning voids. Every missing piece is a chance to claw back compound advantage.

Next, recognize scale relativity. A $10,000 home-equity line may feel minor, but if recycled through a cash-on-cash 20 % micro-asset, it mirrors the function of a $10 million credit facility for a hotel acquisition. Same mechanics, different commas. Find the smallest viable version of each elite strategy—cost segregation on a duplex, a Regulation CF stake in a start-up, a Wyoming LLC for your freelance coding gigs—and execute. **Small proofs de-mythologize the system.**

Finally, adopt a relentless habit of **rule-book reading**. Skim Congressional bill summaries, follow tax-court Twitter feeds, and subscribe to your state's legislative tracker. When new incentives drop—bonus depreciation, energy credits, opportunity zones—be among the first to interpret them through the lens of your budding structure. You will compete not with billionaires, but with peers still waiting for headline news.

Yes, the board is tilted. But the rigging is visible, the angles measurable. Your task is not to demand a flatter board; it is to master balance on the incline until gravity itself becomes your ally.

Mindset + Structure = Escape

Mindset is the software upgrade; **structure** is the hardware install. Run one without the other and the system crashes or idles. Together they form a self-reinforcing engine capable of lifting you out of wage gravity.

Mindset expansion. Shift your internal question set from "How do I earn more?" to "How do I convert earnings into owned systems?" See taxes not as a civic inevitability but as an efficiency puzzle: every line item invites either ignorant payment or informed mitigation. Recast risk: the danger is not starting a tiny holding company—the danger is working 40 years under your SSN with zero shields. Envy becomes obsolete; imitation replaces resentment. You don't begrudge a peer's duplex—you copy the depreciation schedule and hunt for two more units.

Structural scaffolding. Begin with the thin edge of the wedge: a single-member LLC costs less than a weekend trip yet reroutes income to a Schedule C where home-office, phone, and mileage convert into deductible fuel for future capital. Stack an S-corp election when profits justify payroll arbitrage. Add a disregarded LLC beneath a living trust to separate rental property liability from personal residence equity. Each layer is a keystone for the next: merchant processing under the LLC qualifies you for 0 % financing offers; those offers purchase inventory that flows through cost-of-goods-sold deductions; free cash then funds the trust's contribution to a self-directed retirement account that lends back to the LLC on secured notes—loop closed, dollars insulated.

Over time, **compounding differentials appear**. A tax-sheltered dollar reinvested at 15 % grows 40 % faster than an after-tax dollar at 10 %. An entity with pristine books accesses bank money at 6 % when a sole proprietor pays 15 %. A trust bypasses probate fees and public scrutiny, letting heirs redeploy capital months—or years—sooner. These percentage points and calendar gaps sound modest; spread across decades, they redefine dynastic trajectories.

Implementation roadmap:

1. **Quarter One** – File first entity. Open business banking. Isolate operating cash.

2. **Quarter Two** – Draft basic estate docs; designate beneficiaries; secure umbrella liability insurance.

3. **Quarter Three** – Acquire or create your first leveraged asset (small rental, digital product, vending route).

4. **Quarter Four** – Audit taxes with a specialist; deploy the first advanced election or credit (e.g., Section 199A, R&D).

Repeat annually, increasing complexity only as capacity grows. Soon your spreadsheets resemble those of a modest family office. You will notice a psychological flip: instead of saying, "I can't afford that strategy yet," you will ask, "Which line of my structure does this new strategy plug into?"

The elite's apparent magic is simply **architecture disciplined by perspective**. Install the perspective; raise the architecture. Then let compound time perform the escape.

What You Do With This Information Will Define Your Legacy

In every era, a tiny fraction of people learn how money works, while the rest march along well-lit roads designed by someone else. You're now standing at the fork where those roads diverge. One path loops reliably through 40 years of earned-income taxation, inflation erosion, probate delays, and forced asset sales to cover end-of-life costs. The other path is foggier at first—filled with legal terminology, entity documents, and new habits—but it leads to compound advantages that echo long after you are gone. Your choice, made in the next few months, determines which story your balance sheet tells a decade from now.

Don't let the perfect plan sabotage your first move. The wealthy families profiled in this book did not spring fully formed from trust-law textbooks. They made incremental upgrades: a single-shelf corporation here, a basic living trust there, and one cost-seg study on a duplex. Each upgrade unlocked a new lever—better credit terms, reduced audit risk, and larger deductions. Momentum followed. You can copy that cadence immediately.

Start by documenting a 12-month "structure sprint." Month 1: file an LLC for any freelance or side revenue. Month 2: open separate checking and credit lines under the LLC, migrating recurring expenses. Month 3: schedule a strategy session with a CPA who understands S-corp payroll optimization. Month 4: draft a basic will and living trust—even if your only major asset is a car. Months 5–6: identify one asset class—notes, vending routes, digital products—and deploy a sub-$5,000 experiment focused on cash yield, not prestige. By Month 12, you'll own an income stream, an entity lattice, and a taste of how leverage feels in your favor.

Every small step rewires your family narrative. When your children see profits deposited to a company account, and then watch you reinvest those profits into another micro-asset, they internalize ownership as normal. That behavioral inheritance is more valuable than any college fund. You're not just earning dollars; you're creating scripts—mental macros that will replay decades later.

Legacy also means protecting the downside no one talks about: lawsuits, medical events, partner disputes, or sudden regime changes in tax law. Without shields, a single judgment can vaporize 20 years of savings. With even primitive shields—umbrella insurance, a charging-order-protected LLC, a domestic asset-protection trust—you transform from a juicy contingency target into a dry stone. Predators pass you by and look for easier prey.

Do not underestimate the signaling power of early structure. Bankers, brokers, and potential partners measure seriousness by paperwork hygiene. A clean cap table, consistent minutes, and reconciled QuickBooks reports will get you to "yes" faster than charisma or a viral pitch deck. Even if your venture launches with $1,000, institutional-grade discipline forces bigger players to treat you as a peer rather than a hobbyist.

As you advance, keep a simple scorecard:

1. **Entities created**
2. **Income streams detached from labor**
3. **Tax dollars legally redirected**
4. **Assets insulated from personal liability**
5. **Relationships seeded inside higher rooms—lawyers, brokers, operators**

Review the scorecard quarterly. Celebrate micro-wins: your first K-1, your first bank loan at business rates, your first vendor NET-30 account. Those markers prove you're migrating from consumer to architect.

Remember, every dollar that bypasses confiscatory tax, every asset wrapped in a protective veil, every contract that tilts odds toward you—these stack like bricks in a dynasty wall. Future heirs will not remember how many hours you clocked at a job; they will live inside the fortress that your structural choices built.

Yet none of this is guaranteed. If today's motivation dissolves into tomorrow's routine, the opportunity closes. Inflation, policy drift, and market cycles will punish delay. You don't need to predict the future; you need frameworks that thrive in multiple futures—trusts that outlast administrations, assets that cash flow through recessions, privacy layers that endure data leaks, and social volatility.

You now possess the raw code:

Taxes can be optional when income is recharacterized.

Ownership attracts liability; control without title deflects it.

Privacy is a moat, not a moral failing.

Visible wealth invites tolls; shadow wealth compounds toll-free.
Capital flows to structure the way water flows downhill.

The next paragraph of your story is blank. Will you scribble familiar lines—clock in, pay full freight, consume what's left? Or will you draft a new stanza—invisible pipelines, leveraged acquisitions, heirs who inherit frameworks instead of problems?

Re-read any section of this book that sparked curiosity, and then execute its smallest actionable step within 48 hours. File one form, schedule one call, and segregate one account. That micro-commitment breaks inertia. The second step will cost half the effort, and the tenth step will feel inevitable.

Quietly recalibrate your metrics of success: not salary size, but equity percentage; not annual tax paid, but tax legally avoided; not conspicuous consumption, but discreet control. Let friends post pay-raise screenshots; you'll review trust-balance statements. Let influencers flaunt leased supercars; you'll collateralize policy loans at 3 % and redeploy into private credit yielding 14 %—unseen, uninterrupted.

Most readers will close this book, nod appreciatively, and re-enter the scripted game. A few—perhaps you—will realize the door is already ajar. The hardware store of legal entities, strategic debt, and protective jurisdictions is open to anyone literate enough to walk the aisles.

Choose deliberate action over passive outrage. Choose architecture over hope. Choose the quiet confidence that comes from knowing your assets earn, protect, and replicate themselves even while you sleep. That choice, repeated in small increments, redefines not only your net worth but the economic launchpad you hand to the next generation.

Your legacy isn't a will drafted at age seventy; it begins with the contract you sign this week, the entity you file next month, the habit you set for life. Decide now that the rules exposed in these pages will not stay theory—they will become the operating system of your family line.

Move quietly. Move strategically. Move now.

Recap for Essential Information

Fork in the Road
- **Tiny minority:** learns how money works
- **Majority:** follows pre-paved, well-lit roads built by others
- **Two trajectories:**
  1. **Default loop** – 40 years of wages ⇒ income tax ⇒ inflation drags ⇒ probate delays ⇒ forced asset sales
  2. **Foggy corridor** – legal terms, entity filings, new habits ⇒ compounding advantages far beyond your lifetime
- **Decision window:** next few months; outcome visible on your balance sheet ten years ahead

Ignore "Perfect Plan" Paralysis
- Elite wealth was built **incrementally**
  - Shelf corporation → better credit
  - Simple living trust → probate shortcut
  - One cost-seg study → massive deduction
- Each tweak unlocked **cheaper capital + lower audit risk + bigger write-offs**
- Copy the cadence; aim for steady momentum, not flawless blueprints

12-Month "Structure Sprint"

Month	Action	Rationale
1	File LLC for any freelance side money	Liability shield + biz deductions
2	Open biz checking + credit lines	Separate cash flow; start credit DNA
3	Meet CPA on S-corp salary splits	Future payroll-tax arbitrage
4	Draft will + living trust	Estate control even with minor

Month	Action	Rationale
		assets
5–6	Pick **one** asset class (notes, vending, digital)	Deploy <$ 5k for yield experiment
7–9	Reinvest profits via the entity	Compound in sheltered lane
10–12	Review leverage capacity; add an umbrella policy	Risk buffer + borrowing firepower

Behavioral Inheritance

- Kids watch **company deposits** → see ownership as "normal"
- Profits reinvested into micro-assets become scripts they'll replay later
- **System thinking** > one-off windfalls

Downside Shields

- Threats: lawsuits, illness, partner fallout, policy swings
- Basic armor:
  - Umbrella Insurance
  - Charging-order-protected LLC
  - Domestic asset-protection trust
- Goal: transform from "juicy target" → "dry stone"

Early-Structure Signaling

- Professionals judge seriousness by paperwork hygiene
- Clean cap table + reconciled books = faster "yes" from banks and PE shops
- Even with $ 1k start-up cash, institutional discipline earns peer status

Quarterly Scorecard

1. **Entities** formed
2. **Income streams** detached from time
3. **Tax dollars** legally redirected
4. **Assets** ring-fenced from personal liability
5. **High-room relationships** nurtured (lawyers, brokers, operators)

Celebrate micro-wins: first K-1, first bank loan at biz rates, first vendor Net-30. Proof you're shifting from **consumer** → **architect**.

Compound Bricks in a Dynasty Wall

- Every untaxed dollar, every protected asset, every favorably worded contract = one more **brick**
- Heirs won't remember your overtime; they'll live inside the fortress you're building

Urgency Over Prediction

- Delay invites inflation, legislative change, recessions
- Build **future-proof frameworks:**
    - Trusts survive politics
    - Cash-flow assets ride cycles
    - Privacy layers outlast data leaks

Raw Code Recap

- Tax ≈ optional when income is re-characterized
- The title invites lawsuits; **control without a title** deflects them
- Privacy = defensive moat, not wrongdoing
- Flashy balance sheets pay tolls; **shadow wealth** compounds toll-free
- Capital gravitates to well-designed structures like water downhill

- Keep scripting: salary → tax → leftovers → consumption
- Or the author's new stanza: invisible pipelines, leveraged buys, heirs inheriting **frameworks** not problems

48-Hour Micro-Commitment

1. File **one** form
2. Book **one** professional call
3. Segregate **one** account

Break inertia; each subsequent action requires half the effort.

Success KPI Shift

- **Old:** salary size, tax paid, visible luxuries
- **New:** equity %, tax legally avoided, discreet control

Open-Door Reality

- The "hardware store" of entities, credit, and jurisdictions stands open for anyone literate enough to browse the aisles.

Final Directive

- **Pick architecture over outrage**
- Let assets **earn, shield, and replicate** while you sleep
- Legacy starts **now**—with this week's contract, next month's entity, lifelong habit formation

Move quietly. Move strategically. **Move now.**

www.ingramcontent.com/pod-product-compliance
Lightning Source LLC
Chambersburg PA
CBHW072159160426
43197CB00012B/2454